Children's Worship Activities

Year 2

Compiled by
Virginia Kessen

Abingdon Press

Children's Worship Activities

Year 2

Activities are taken from *New Invitation One Room Sunday School,* © 1994-1996, Cokesbury; *One Room Sunday School,* © 1997-2002, Abingdon Press; *Children's Worship Activity Sheets,* © 1998, Cokesbury.

ISBN 0-687-02828-0

02 03 04 05 06 07 08 09 10 11 - 10 9 8 7 6 5 4 3 2 1

MANUFACTURED IN THE UNITED STATES OF AMERICA

Color the diamonds ◇ yellow.

Color the triangles △ green.

Color the rectangles ▯ purple.

Do you recognize one way we prepare for Jesus' birthday?

Traditions! Traditions! Traditions

Traditions are customs that are passed from generation to generation. Cultures have traditions; groups have traditions; families have traditions. Important values, beliefs, and ideas are passed on through traditions. Traditions help people remember and celebrate the things that are important to them.

What are the Advent and Christmas traditions in your family?

What Advent and Christmas traditions are celebrated in your church?

What new Advent and Christmas traditions would you like to start?

Put this list with your Christmas card list or with your tree decorations. Then when you find the list next year, you will be reminded of special traditions to continue.

DOT-TO-DOT
1
2
3
4
5
6
7
8
9
10
11
12
13
14
15

Who Is John the Baptist?

John the Baptist spent many days in the wilderness considering the task that God had called him for. Use the nine clues and the pictures of the animals around the page to discover a word that describes what God called John to be.

___ 1. The last letter in the name of the animal that is a male sheep.

___ 2. The second letter in the name of the animal with antlers.

___ 3. The first letter in the name of the reptile that stays cool.

___ 4. The fifth letter in the name of the animal that is similar to a grasshopper.

___ 5. The third letter in the name of the animal that flies.

___ 6. The second letter in the name of the animal that is long and has no legs.

___ 7. The first letter in the name of the animal that has a "beard."

___ 8. The second letter in the name of the animal that makes wild honey.

___ 9. The fourth letter in the name of the animal that has four pairs of legs.

Ram

Bees

DEER

Goat

Snake

Locust

Scorpion

Now read Mark 1:6. Name two things John wore and two things John ate.

John wore ________________ and ________________.

John ate ________________ and ________________.

Answers on page 123

Can you match each promise with the picture of the promise fulfilled?

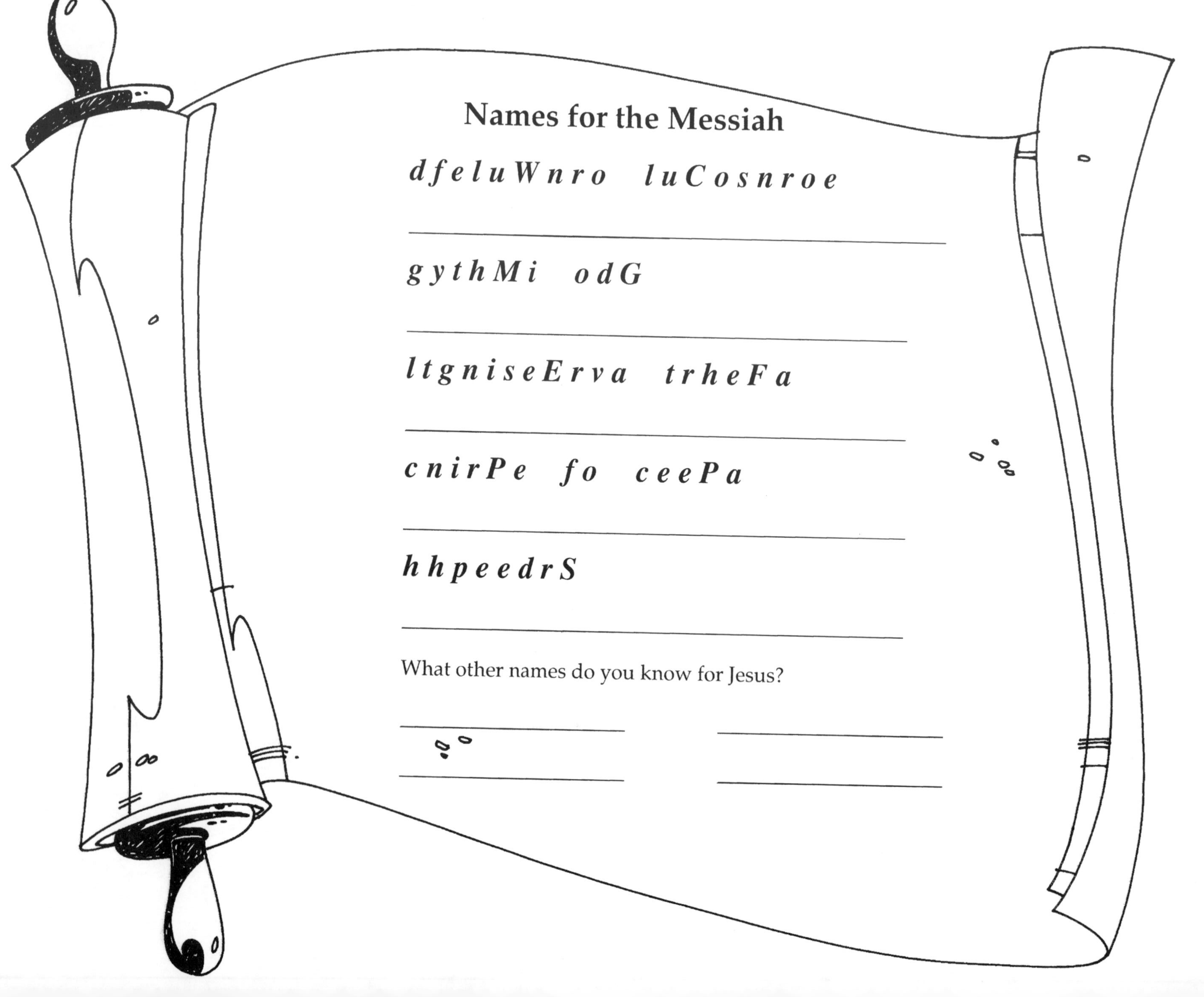

Names for the Messiah

d f e l u W n r o   l u C o s n r o e

____

g y t h M i   o d G

____

l t g n i s e E r v a   t r h e F a

____

c n i r P e   f o   c e e P a

____

h h p e e d r S

____

What other names do you know for Jesus?

______________   ______________

______________   ______________

Answers on page 123

Match the baby items that Mary used in Bible times with the items a mother would use for a baby today.

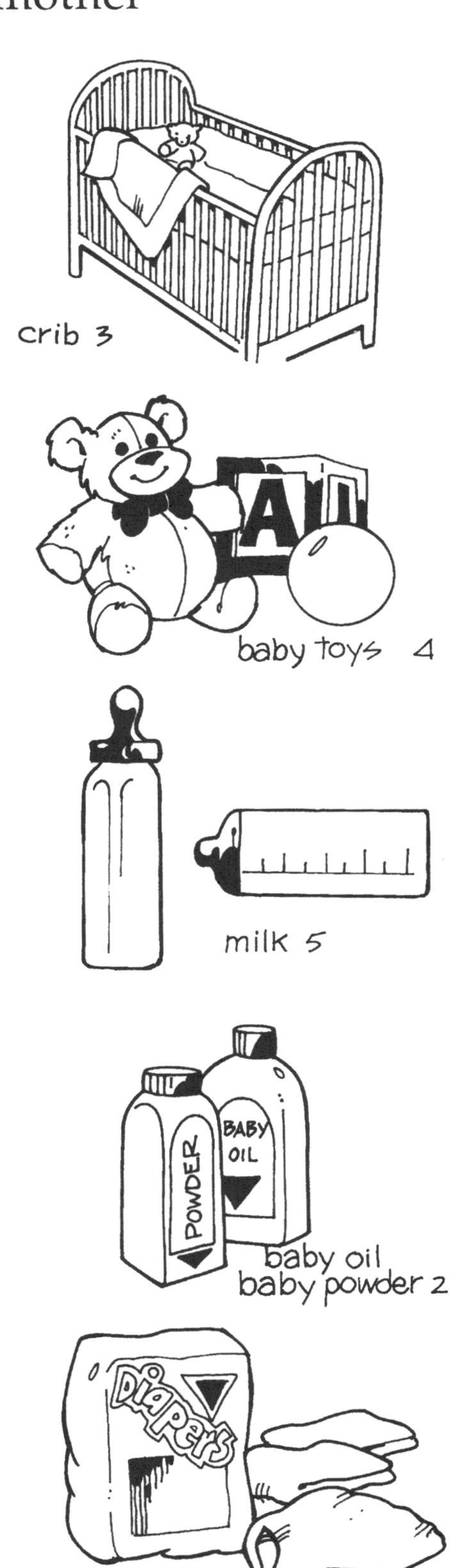

When Gabriel told Mary she would have a son, Mary did not know how that would be possible. Put the letters from the Christmas tree in order on the lines below to find out how Gabriel answered Mary. Find Luke 1:37 to check your answer.

_ _ _ _ _ _ _ _ _ _ _ _ _ _ _ _ _

_ .

Luke 1:37

Where's Baby Jesus?

Can you find baby Jesus? Draw a circle around Jesus' picture.

What Did the Shepherds Tell?

Fill in the missing letters in the words below. If you need help, find and read Luke 2:15-18 in your Bible.

"Let's ☐o now," the shepherds said to
☐ne another. "Let's go to Bethlehem."
s☐ they went quickly, and they
foun☐ Mary and Joseph and the child, who was lying in the manger.
Whe☐ the shepherds saw this, they
mad☐ known what had been told them about this child.
All ☐ho heard it were amazed at what
the ☐hepherds told them.

Reading down, what do the letters you filled in spell?__________________________

Who is the good news about?__________________________

Answers on page 123

Step 1: Color and cut out all pictures.
Step 2: Mary and Joseph are going to stand up and be a two-sided picture. Glue together so that you have a front and back view. Use glue stick, not liquid glue.
Step 3: Fold picture of Mary and Joseph in half. Fold tabs as indicated on pattern.
Step 4: Fold Temple in half. Fold tabs as indicated on dotted lines.
Step 5: Fold a sheet of construction paper in half to make a card.
Step 6: Place Temple and Nicanor Gate on construction paper card. Fold on dotted lines. All tabs must be folded the same direction. Glue or tape in place. Temple goes at top of page. Nicanor Gate goes next.
Step 7: Simeon and Anna attach to gate.
Step 8: Fold tabs for Simeon and Anna on dotted lines. They form a square. Glue square tabs behind Simeon and Anna. Glue or tape to Nicanor Gate and card. Use only glue stick or tape.

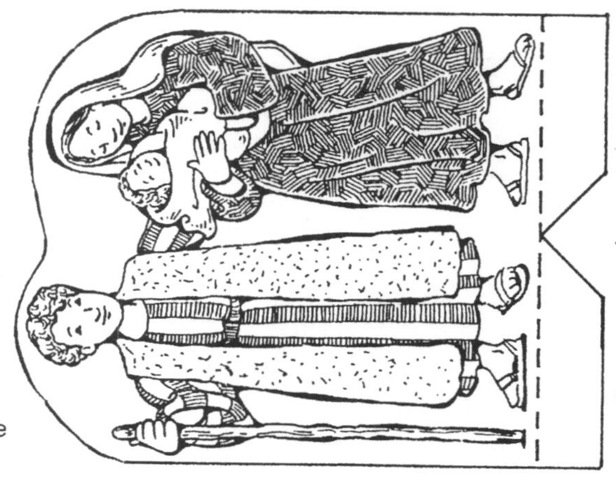

Step 9: Leave some space between pictures. Mary and Joseph go in front of Anna and Simeon.
Step 10: Entire scene should close and pop-up when opened.

Camel Maze

The Wise Men

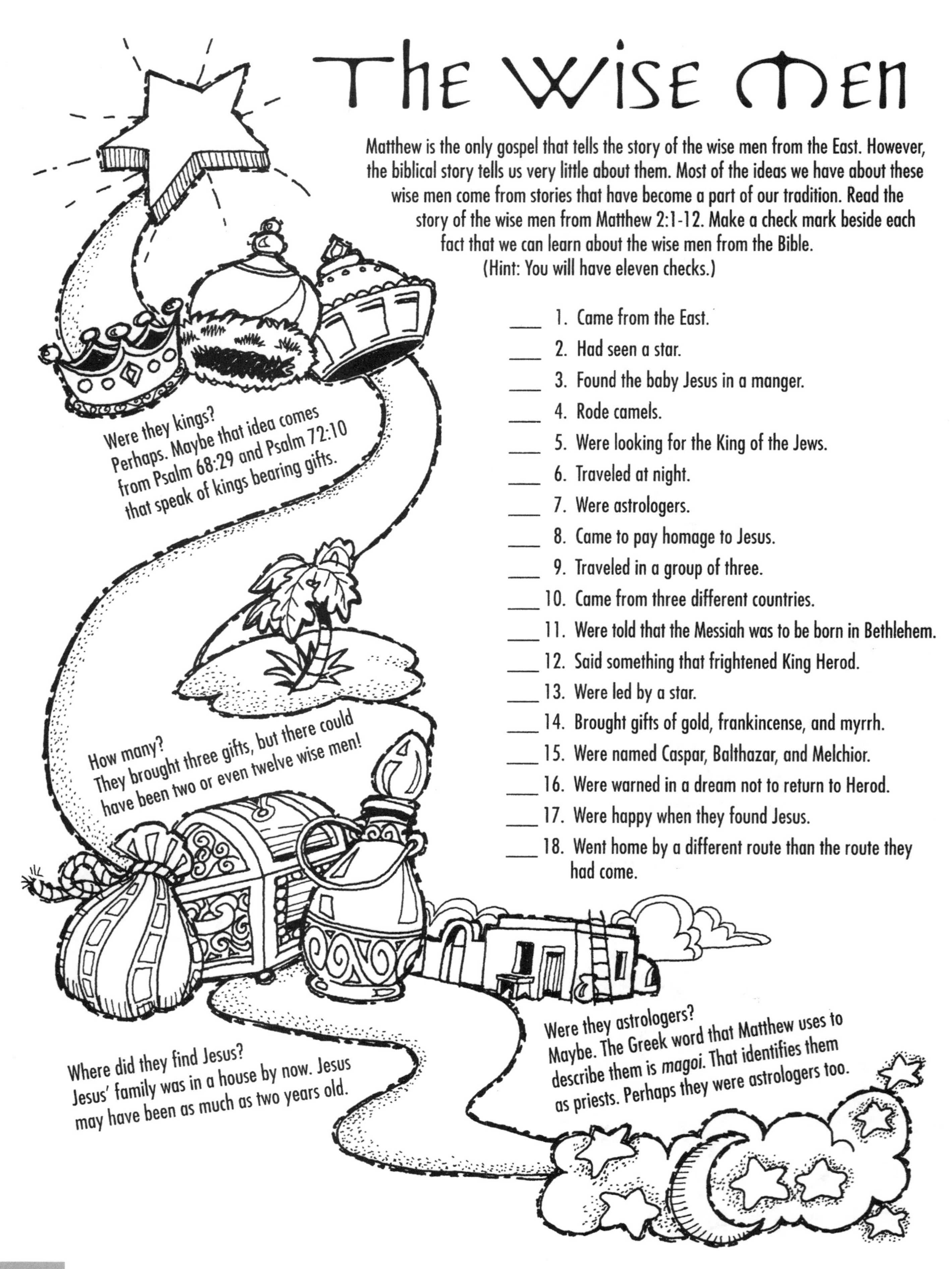

Matthew is the only gospel that tells the story of the wise men from the East. However, the biblical story tells us very little about them. Most of the ideas we have about these wise men come from stories that have become a part of our tradition. Read the story of the wise men from Matthew 2:1-12. Make a check mark beside each fact that we can learn about the wise men from the Bible.
(Hint: You will have eleven checks.)

___ 1. Came from the East.
___ 2. Had seen a star.
___ 3. Found the baby Jesus in a manger.
___ 4. Rode camels.
___ 5. Were looking for the King of the Jews.
___ 6. Traveled at night.
___ 7. Were astrologers.
___ 8. Came to pay homage to Jesus.
___ 9. Traveled in a group of three.
___ 10. Came from three different countries.
___ 11. Were told that the Messiah was to be born in Bethlehem.
___ 12. Said something that frightened King Herod.
___ 13. Were led by a star.
___ 14. Brought gifts of gold, frankincense, and myrrh.
___ 15. Were named Caspar, Balthazar, and Melchior.
___ 16. Were warned in a dream not to return to Herod.
___ 17. Were happy when they found Jesus.
___ 18. Went home by a different route than the route they had come.

This is my Son,
...with whom
I am well pleased.
Matthew 3:17

Ways to Baptize

1. Begin with the letter at the arrow.
2. Go around the circle clockwise two times, writing every other letter on the line above the puzzle.
3. Erase the last letter.
4. Divide the remaining letters to make three words.
5. Write each word on the line below the method of baptism pictured.

Draw a Prayer

Messages From God

God called Samuel. The Bible tells many other stories of people who were called by God.

1. Find each story in your Bible.
2. Draw a line from the Bible reference to the words that God spoke.
3. Then write the name of the person who was called by God with the words.
4. What is God calling you to do? Fill in the last blank.

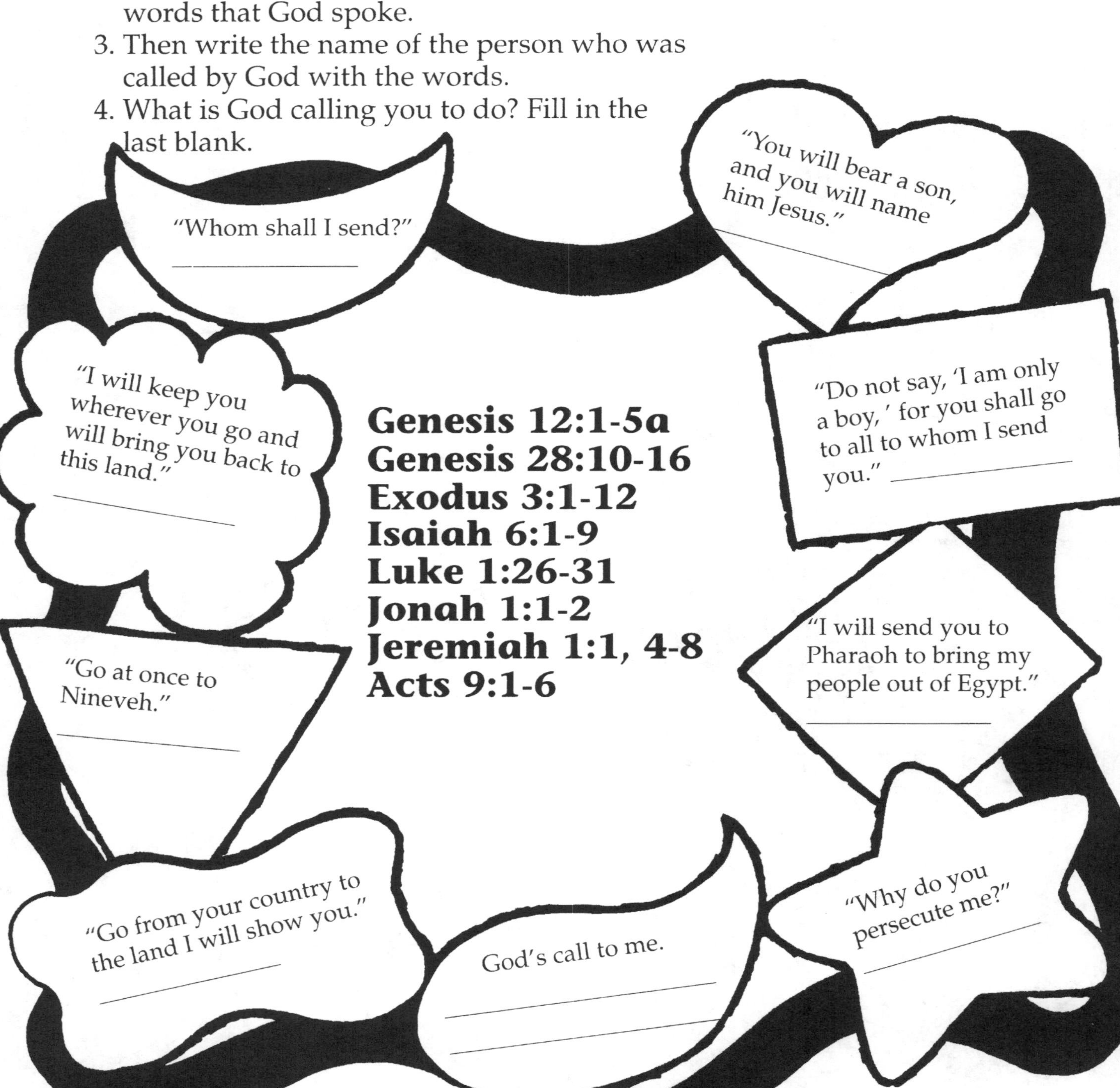

Answers on page 123

1. Choose one fish.
2. Find a second fish exactly like the one fish you have chosen.
3. Color the two fish the same color.
4. Choose a third fish. Then find a matching fish. Color these two fish a second color.
5. Continue until all the matching pairs of fish are a different color.
How many pairs of matching fish can you find?

Jonah finally obeyed God and went to Nineveh. In Nineveh, Jonah delivered a message for God.

Follow Jonah from Start through the streets of Nineveh. Each time you come to a word along the path that runs from one side of the city to the other side, write the word on the line below the picture. Watch out for dead ends!

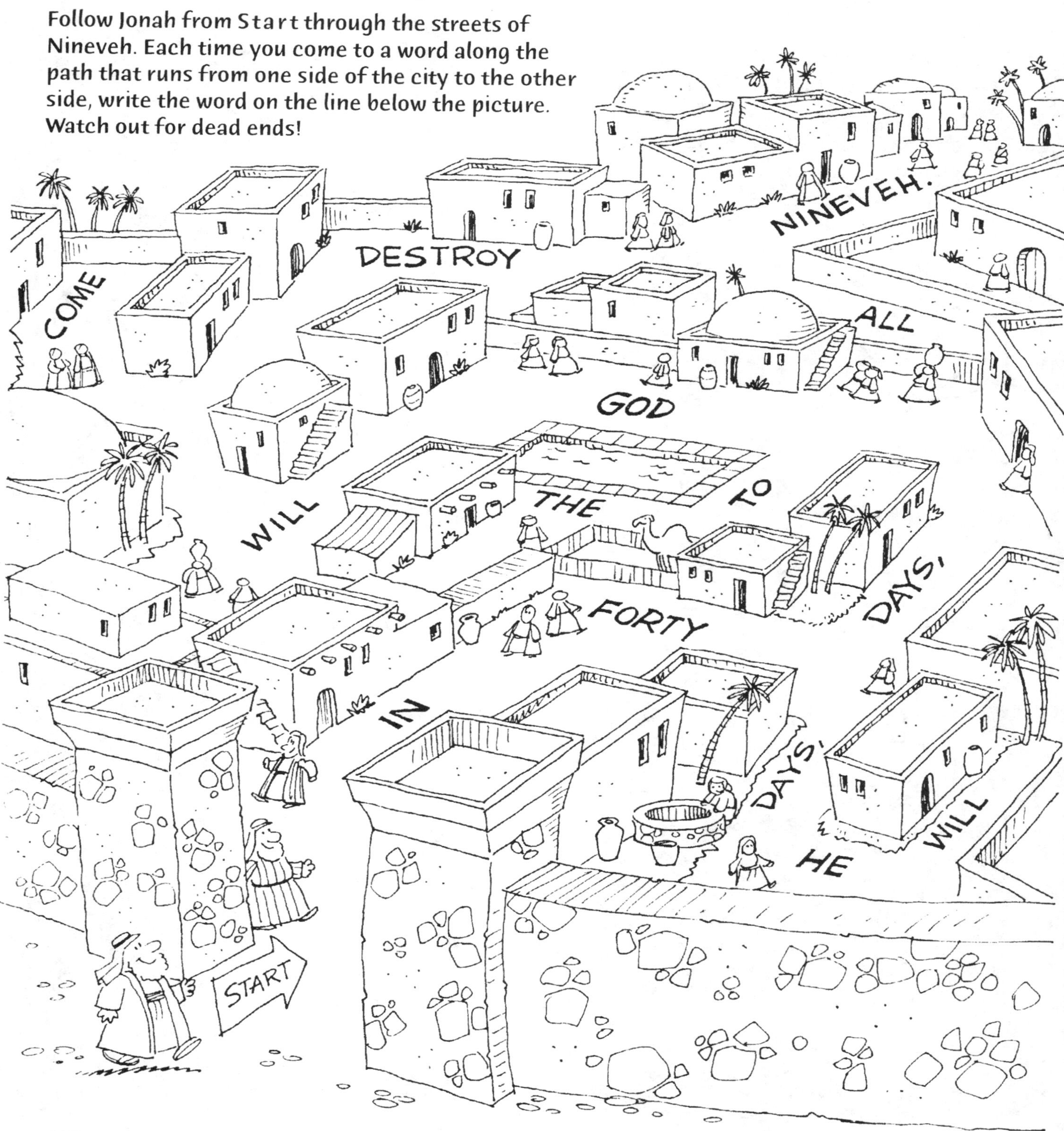

What message did Jonah deliver?

____

When Jesus called the first disciples, "they left everything and followed him."
(Luke 5:11b)

Draw a line to show the path from each disciple to Jesus.

Follow the Leader

Across

2. Sold purple cloth (Acts 16:14)
3. A tax collector (Matthew 9:9)
7. Brother of James (Matthew 4:21)
9. Welcomed Jesus into her home (Luke 10:38)
11. Wept at Jesus' tomb (John 20:1, 11)
14. Betrayed Jesus with kiss (Mark 14:43-46)
16. Called a Zealot (Luke 6:15)
17. Denied Jesus three times (Mark 14:72)
18. His Hebrew name was Saul (Acts 26:1, 14)
20. Provided for Jesus (Luke 8:3)
21. Heard about Jesus from Philip (John 1:45)
22. Provided for Jesus (Luke 8:3)

Down

1. Wife of Aquila; tentmaker (Acts 18:2-3)
4. Was called "the Twin" (John 20:24)
5. Mother of Jesus (Luke 1:30-31)
6. Maid who welcomed Peter (Acts 12:13-14)
7. Brother of John, son of Zebedee (Mark 1:19)
8. Another name for the disciple called Nathanael in John 1:47, begins with the letter *B* (Matthew 10:3)
10. Another Judas. He was often called by a name that begins with the letter *T*. (Matthew 10:3)
12. Simon Peter's brother (John 1:40-41)
13. Made clothes (Acts 9:39)
15. One of the women who went to anoint Jesus' body (Mark 16:1)
17. Said to Jesus, "Show us the Father." (John 14:8)
19. A missionary with Paul (Acts 13:2-4)

Answers on page 124

Be A Helping Friend

Use a different color crayon to find a way to get each gift to the sick friend in the middle.

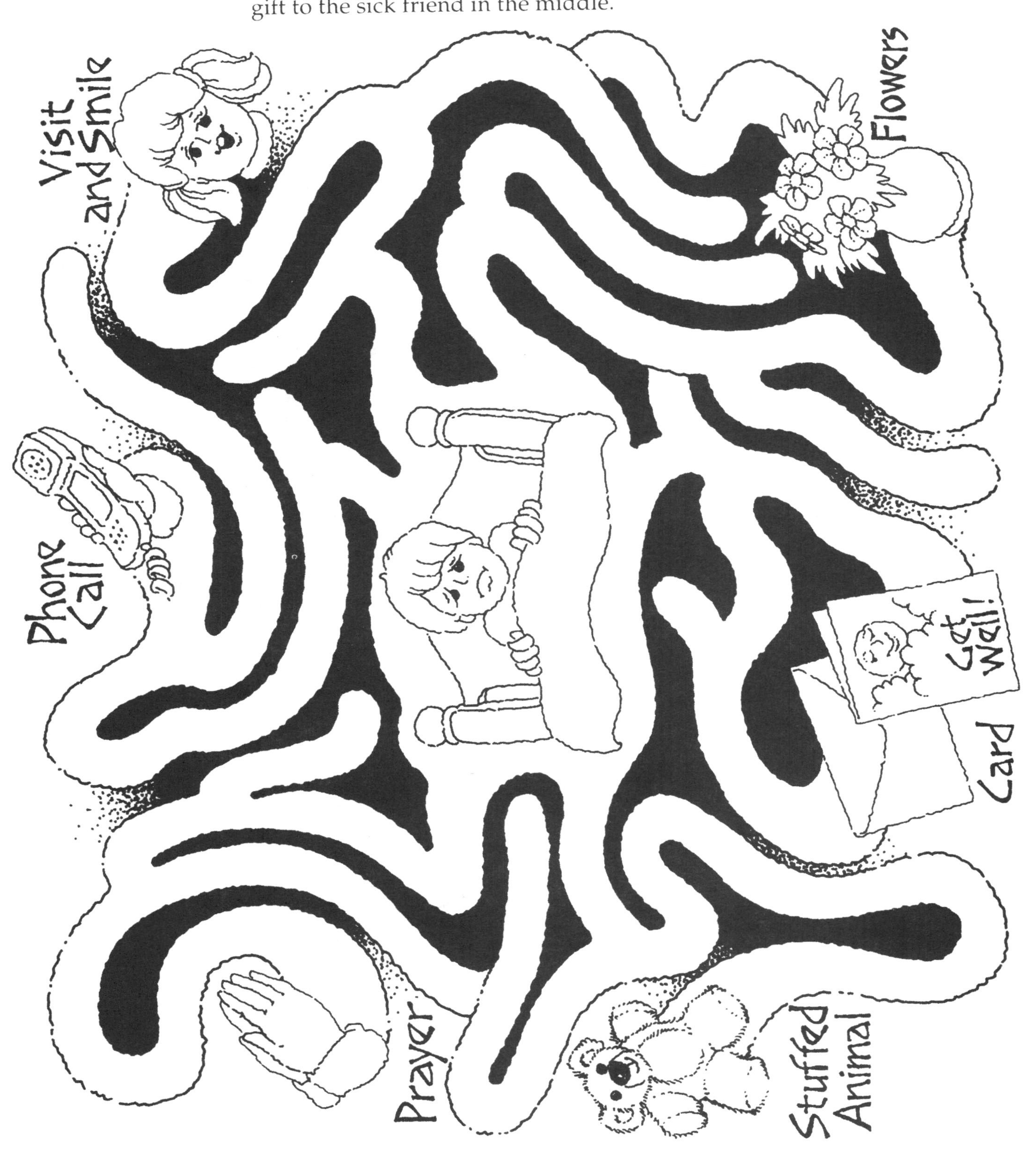

Circle the words below that name ways you can reach out to other people to show them that you care about them.

Compliment	Interact	Ignore	Reject
Speak	Care	Help	Give
Disapprove	Love	Hate	Tattle
Include	Frown	Accept	
Smile	Share	Tease	

Can you add some other words to circle? ____________ ____________

Fill in all the spaces in the letters below that contain *O*'s. Who does Jesus love and want us to reach out to? ______________________

I Y Q J H Y T E C W E T U F C D E W C S W T F E C R D F E W T Y G V E A L Q P J

O O O B O Z A R O X O O O I O O O W S B O B W V O Q O O O Y O U J P O K O O O K

O L B X O V P F O M O K W D O E O C W T R O G O R F O T O B O O U K O M O G H N

O O Y Q N O K O A Z O O L X O O O Y R V K K O Q H Q O S O X O L O E O I O O P G

O Z D M C O N O B J O B E F O I E O C I H W O H X E O A O A O G A O O F O G Z J

O O O P A U O K M T O O O Z O K J L O J R H O B I D O O O U O S R G O C O O O F

D Y N V L Y U Y P N F Y M K N Q L J C V A U L G F Z W V R F D H P S K I H D L Z

Answers on page 124

Jesus taught us to love one another.
Follow the maze.
How are these children showing love?

How do you show love to others?

How many hearts can you find? ___________

Draw a line from each person who is sick or injured to the same person being helped or healed.

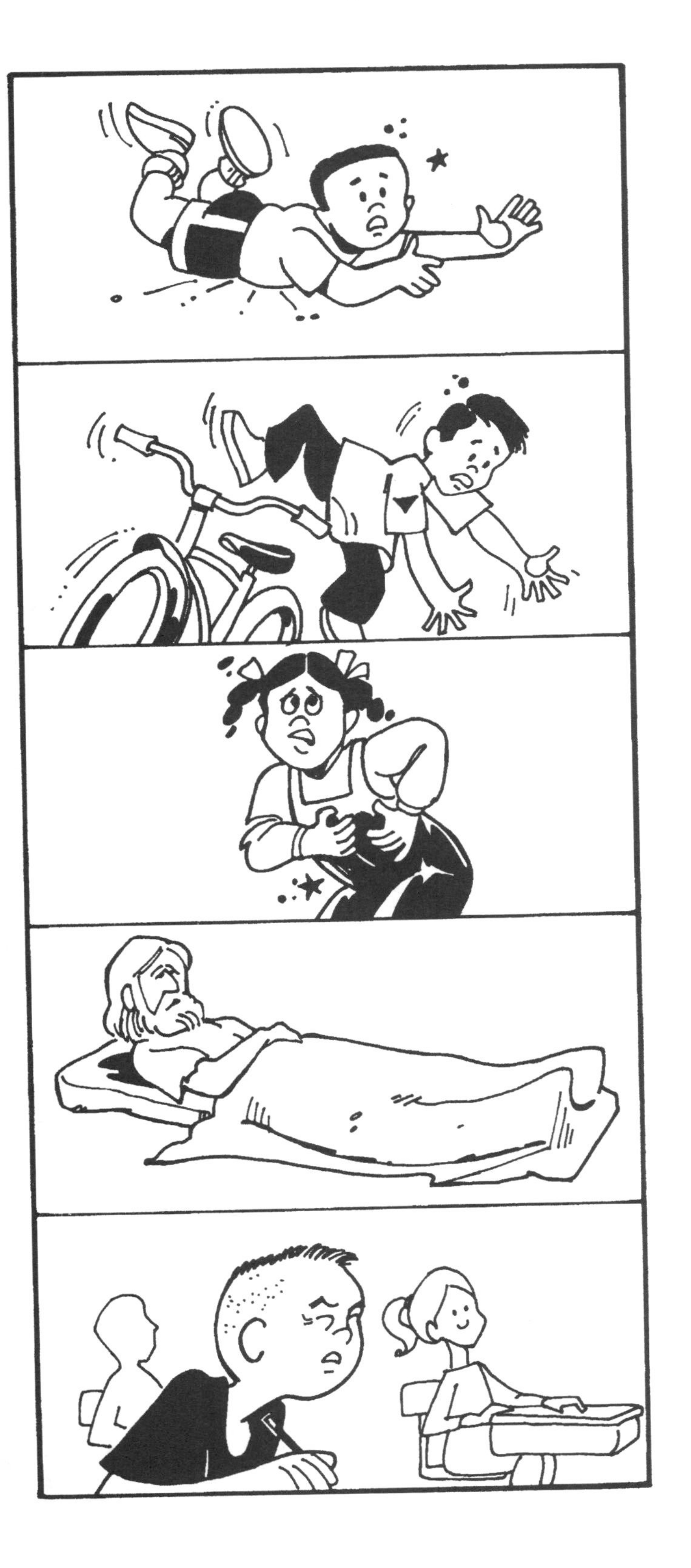

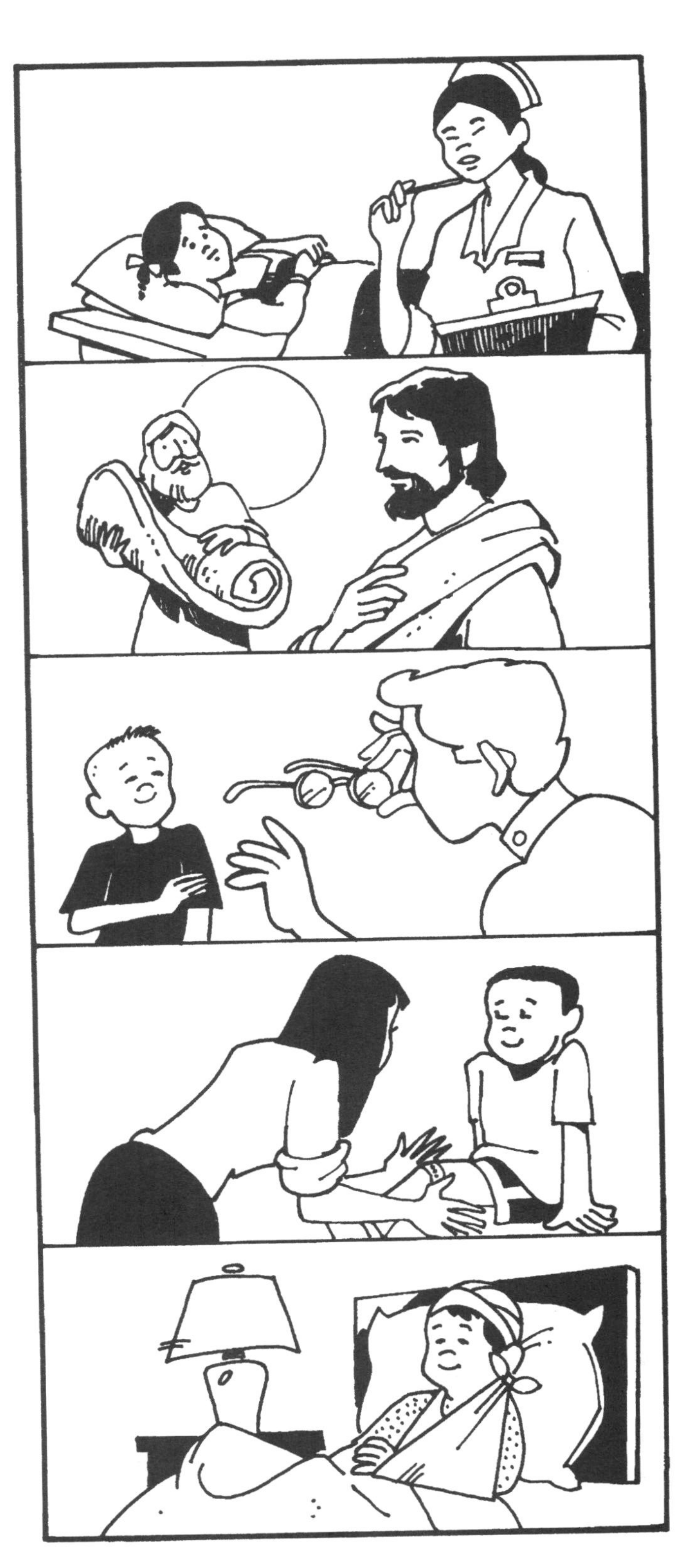

Acquaintances: People we know, but not very well. Acquaintances seldom do things together. Most people have lots of acquaintances.

Some of my acquaintances are

________, ________,

________, ________.

Good Friends: Friends we see often. Good friends plan to play together or to go places together. Most people usually have several good friends.

Some of my good friends are

________, ________, ________

and ________.

Best Friends: Friends who are very close. Best friends see each other or talk to each other often. Best friends talk to each other about the most important things in their lives. Most people usually have only one or two best friends.

My best friends are

____

and ________.

Kinds of Friends
Qualities I Want in a Friend

Acquaintances

____

Good Friends

____

Best Friends

____

Party
TICKET 311007
TICKET 311007
JIM SMITH
BEST Friends Forever!

Litter
Litter
Litter

Color every other stone as you follow the trail.
Write the letters on the lines to discover what God said about Israel and what God still says about us.

_ ______ ______ ______ ______

____ __ ________.

Hosea 14: 4b
(Good News Bible)

Answers on page 124

Name
I am a follower of Jesus

Symbol Scavenger Hunt

Can you find things in your church that remind you of God?

It's purple, and it covers the altar. ______________________

Purple stands for the season of ________________ , which last 40 days.

During worship it has a flame to remind us of God's presence and guidance.

____

It reminds us that Jesus died on Good Friday and was raised from the dead on Easter. Some people wear this symbol as a necklace or a pin. ____________________

It reminds us of the table where Jesus and his disciples ate the Last Supper.

____

What other symbols can you find in your church?

The ___________________________ reminds me

____

The ___________________________ reminds me

____

The ___________________________ reminds me

____

IN REMEMBRANCE OF ME

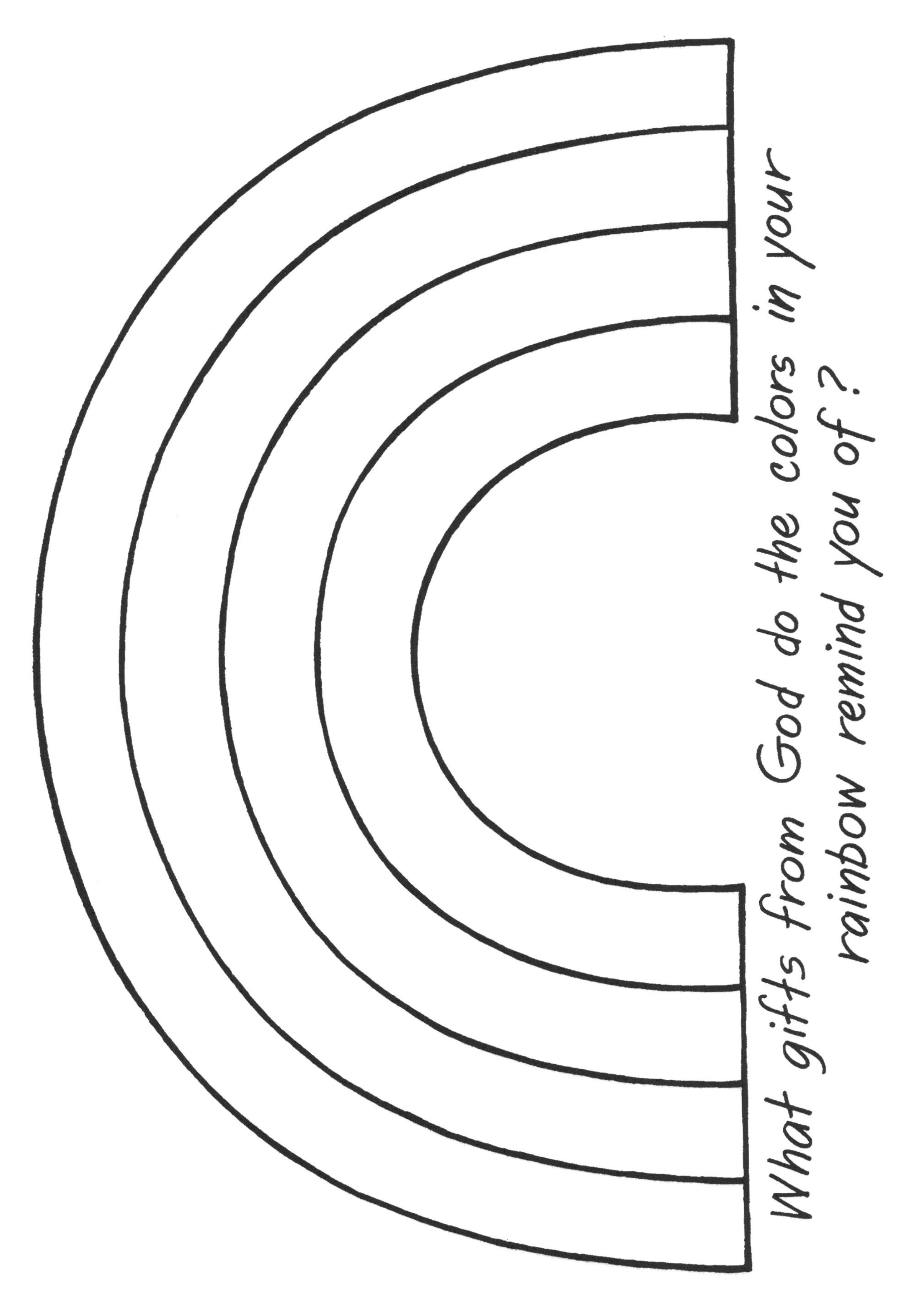
What gifts from God do the colors in your
rainbow remind you of?

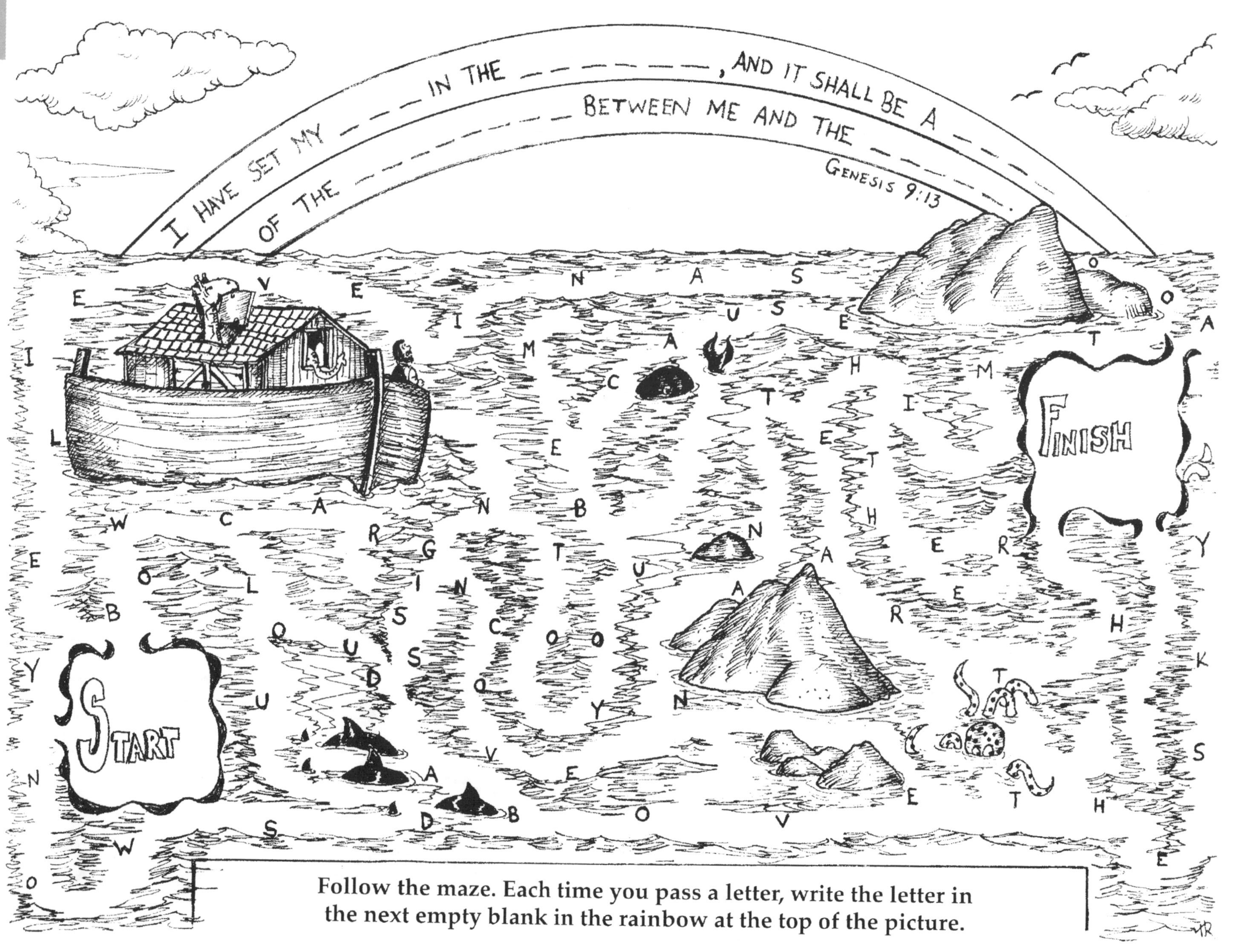

Follow the maze. Each time you pass a letter, write the letter in the next empty blank in the rainbow at the top of the picture.

Then and Now

Match the pictures from Abraham's time and today.

A covenant is an agreement that creates a special relationship. A covenant requires that each of those who make the covenant be faithful to a special promise. God made a covenant with Abraham. Read Genesis 12:1-3 to help you remember the promises each of them made.

God promised Abraham	Abraham promised God

The Covenant Today

The covenant God made with Abraham long before Jesus was born is recorded in the Old Testament.

Read Genesis 17:7.
The covenant was between God, Abraham, and Abraham's
____________________.

The New Testament is about the new covenant God made with all people when Jesus came. (In fact, the word *testament* means covenant!)

Read Galatians 3:26-29 to discover the relationship between God's new covenant through Jesus and the covenant with Abraham in the Old Testament.

If you belong to Christ, then you are

Abraham's ____________________,

heirs according to the

______________. (Galatians 3:29)

The symbol of our acceptance of God's covenant today is baptism. (Galatians 3:27) Through baptism we agree to be faithful to God as Abraham was faithful to God. The sacrament of baptism recognizes us as members of God's family. Have you been baptized? If you were baptized when you were a baby, ask your parents to tell you about it.

One More Thing!

Remember that God gave new names to Abraham and Sarah as a symbol of their new relationship with God. When a person is baptized today, the pastor uses the person's name as part of the baptism sacrament. This symbolic act indicates that through baptism we are people who have a special relationship with God.

BICYCLE RIDERS MUST WEAR HELMETS
DO NOT PICK THE FLOWERS
TRASH
TRASH
TRASH
DO NOT LITTER
DOGS MUST BE ON LEASHES
HOME
10
9
8
7
6
5
4
3
2
1
DO NOT RIDE BICYCLES ON THE GRASS
NO ROUGH PLAY
MEG

The Ten Commandments for Today

Match each commandment with the description of a situation where the commandment influenced someone's decision.

___ 1. You shall have no other gods before me.

___ 2. You shall not make for yourself an idol. You shall not bow down to them or worship them.

___ 3. You shall not make wrongful use of the name of the Lord your God.

___ 4. Remember the sabbath day, and keep it holy.

___ 5. Honor your father and mother.

___ 6. You shall not murder.

___ 7. You shall not commit adultery.

___ 8. You shall not steal.

___ 9. You shall not bear false witness against your neighbor.

___ 10. You shall not covet ... anything that belongs to your neighbor.

a. Even though Sammy did not want to leave the ball game, he respected his parents and got home by the time they had told him to come.

b. Sarah had never been so mad. She found her father's gun in the closet. But when she remembered that God loves every person, she put it back.

c. When Eric asked Jonathan to ride bicycles with him on Sunday morning, Jonathan said, "We will have to wait until after church."

d. Jessica's family couldn't afford the new CD player she wanted, but she was happy for her friend Sally when Sally got a new CD player for her birthday.

e. Bob decided to stop going places with Michael if Michael continued to use God's name in curses.

f. When Betsy's friend tried to get her to hide a candy bar from the store shelf in her pocket, Betsy said, "No."

g. Sondra decided not to join the soccer team because she knew it was more important for her to worship God than to practice on Sunday mornings.

h. Brian thought about getting back at Randy by telling people that Randy had stolen a bicycle, but he decided that saying so would be wrong.

i. Ashley was disappointed when she heard that her aunt was dating a man other than Ashley's uncle.

j. Jason practiced on Sunday morning because winning the trophy was more important to him than going to church. His friends said it was like the trophy was his god.

Answers on page 124

Who does Jesus love?
Jesus loves me!
Jesus loves me!

We show God's love
by how we treat others!

List the promises that are a part of your covenant with God.

On the left side of the heart, write what God has promised to do for you.

On the right side, write the promises you will make to God about being one of God's people.

A covenant is a promise between two people or between God and God's people.

There are many covenants recorded in the Bible. Find each of the covenants listed here in your Bible. Who made each covenant?

Genesis 17:1-8
A covenant between ________ and __________

Genesis 21:25-32
A covenant between ________ and __________

Exodus 34:1-10
A covenant between ________ and __________

Genesis 31:43-46, 51-52
A covenant between ________ and __________

1 Chronicles 11:3
A covenant between ________ and __________

Exodus 19:5-6a
A covenant between ________ and __________

Genesis 9:8-17
A covenant between ________ and __________

Genesis 12:1-2
A covenant between ________ and __________

Psalm 132:11-12
A covenant between ________ and __________

Jeremiah spoke for God when he said that God would make a new covenant with the people. Read Jeremiah 31:31-34. Then write the new covenant from verse 33 here.

____

____

____

____

People have broken their covenants many times. But God's covenant has never been broken.

Answers on page 125

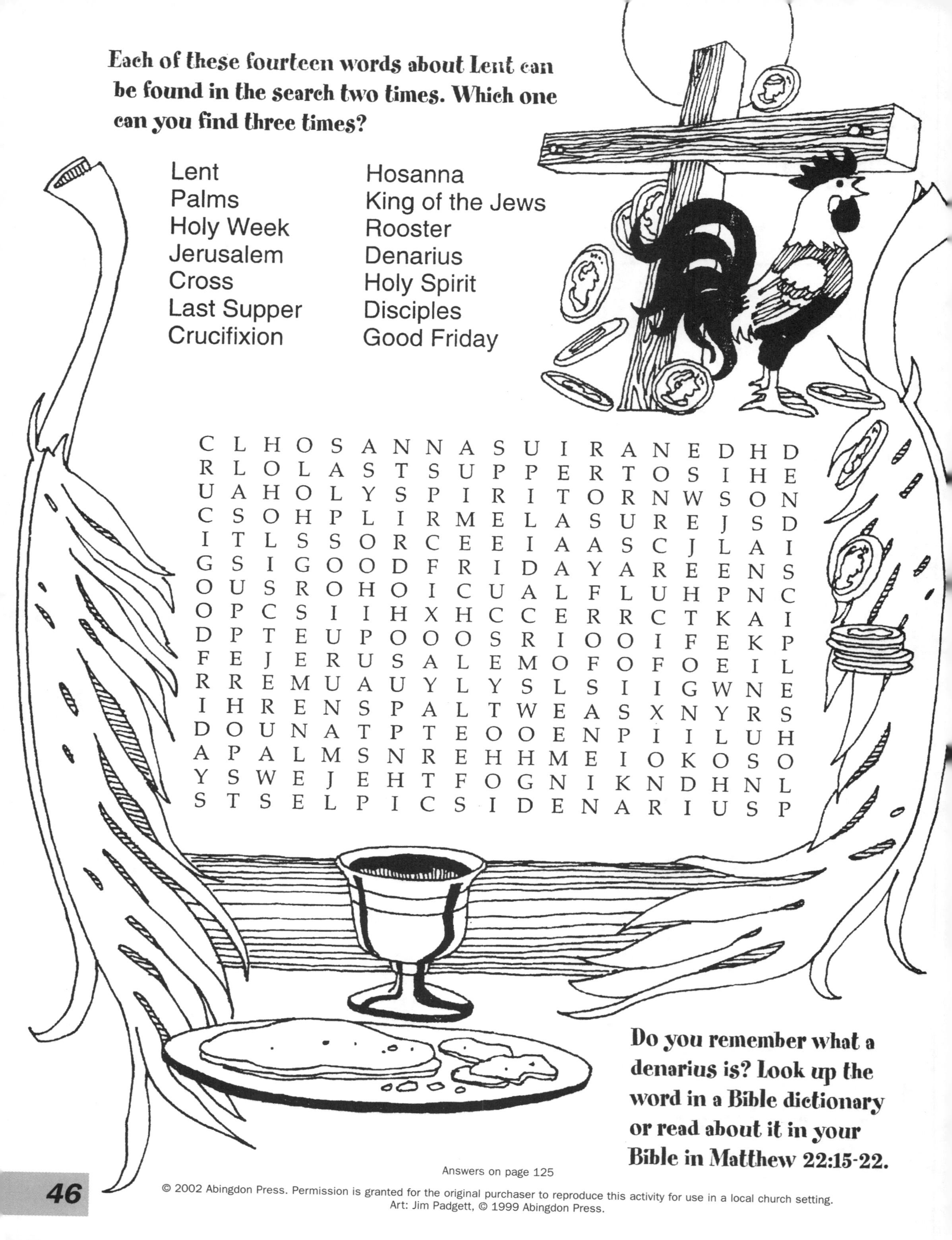

Each of these fourteen words about Lent can be found in the search two times. Which one can you find three times?

Lent	Hosanna
Palms	King of the Jews
Holy Week	Rooster
Jerusalem	Denarius
Cross	Holy Spirit
Last Supper	Disciples
Crucifixion	Good Friday

C L H O S A N N A S U I R A N E D H D
R L O L A S T S U P P E R T O S I H E
U A H O L Y S P I R I T O R N W S O N
C S O H P L I R M E L A S U R E J S D
I T L S S O R C E E I A A S C J L A I
G S I G O O D F R I D A Y A R E E N S
O U S R O H O I C U A L F L U H P N C
O P C S I I H X H C C E R R C T K A I
D P T E U P O O O S R I O O I F E K P
F E J E R U S A L E M O F O F O E I L
R R E M U A U Y L Y S L S I I G W N E
I H R E N S P A L T W E A S X N Y R S
D O U N A T P T E O O E N P I I L U H
A P A L M S N R E H H M E I O K O S O
Y S W E J E H T F O G N I K N D H N L
S T S E L P I C S I D E N A R I U S P

Do you remember what a denarius is? Look up the word in a Bible dictionary or read about it in your Bible in Matthew 22:15-22.

Answers on page 125

Thank you, God, for days to play.

Thank you, God, for our church.

Dear God, thank you for our family. Amen.

How many crosses can you find?

The season of the church year during which we prepare for Easter is called ________ (4 across)

________ (2 down) was the first disciple to recognize that Jesus was the Messiah. Jesus called him a ________ (6 across) and said that the church would be built on this disciple's faith.

The Sunday before Easter, we celebrate the day Jesus arrived in Jerusalem riding on a ________ (3 down). We call that day ________ ________ (9 across), the beginning of ________ ________ (1 down), the time when we remember Jesus' last week.

When Jesus entered Jerusalem, the people shouted ________ (5 across) and waved ________ (7 down).

The religious leaders tried to ________ (12 down) Jesus by asking him whether it was right for the Jews to pay taxes. Jesus told them to give to ________ (14 down) the things that were God's.

At the end of the Last Supper, Jesus promised that the disciples would not be alone after Jesus was gone. God would send the ________ ________ (13 across).

Before Jesus was arrested, he prayed for himself, for the disciples who had been following him, and for all the disciples in the future, including ________ (10 down).

Peter, one of the closest and strongest disciples, was afraid when Jesus was arrested. He denied knowing Jesus ________ (8 down) times on the night Jesus was arrested.

Jesus was tried and sentenced to death on a ________ (11 down).

Even when Jesus was dying, he asked God to ________ (15 across) those who had condemned him.

Answers on page 125

Instructions: Color the window and discover the memory verse and symbols that remind us of Easter.

Begin with the **O** near the top center. Follow the words of Psalm 98:1a, 4 to find an Easter symbol and words of joy that Mary Magdalene might have sung on the first Easter morning.

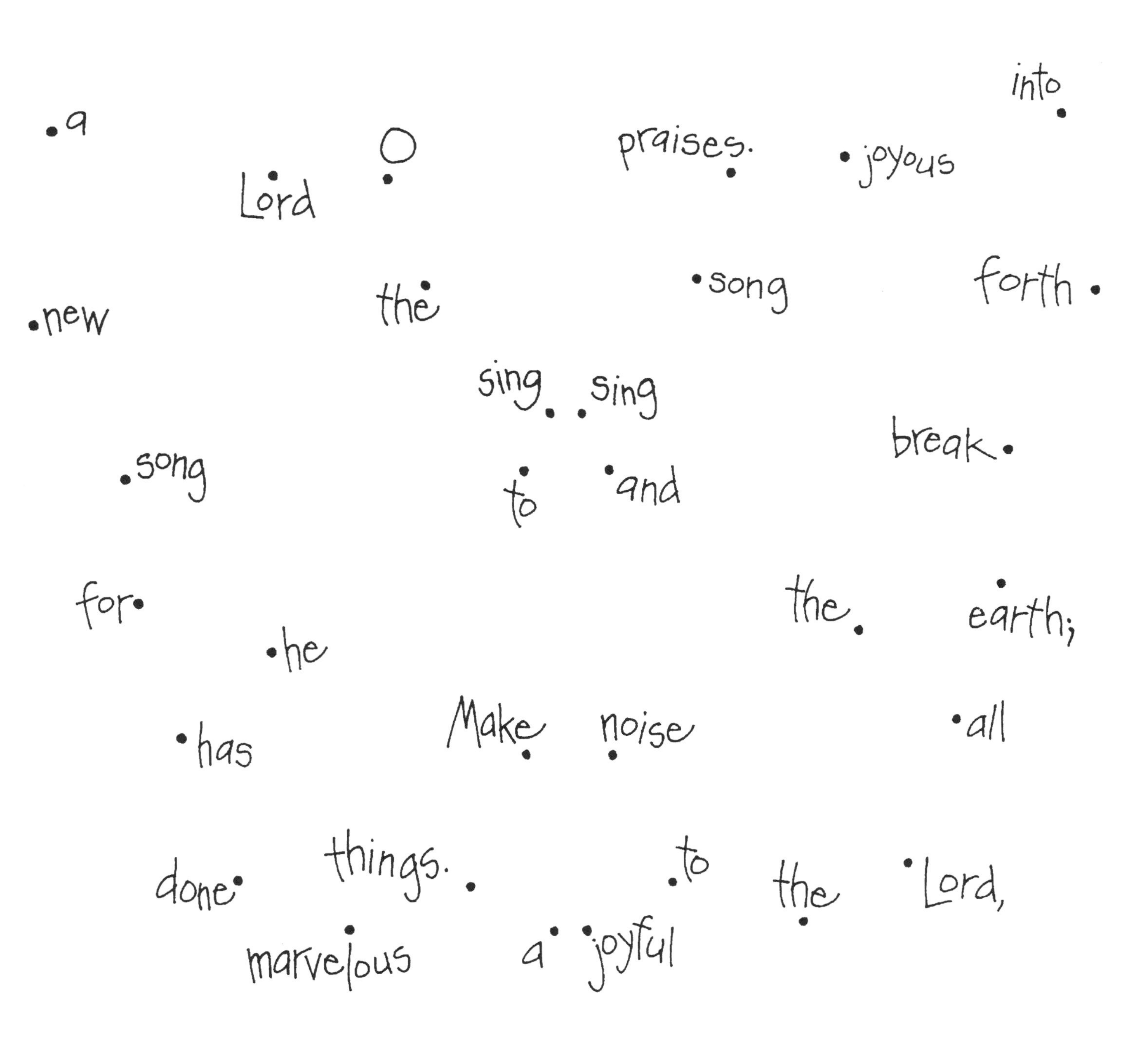

I Can Share

Glue or draw pictures in the gift box that show ways you can share with others.

C.L.U.E.S.

Unscramble the words in each magnifying glass to discover the ways that

Caring Lights Up Everyone's Spring!

Use the C.L.U.E.S. to solve the mystery of Christian growth.

This week I can use my __________ to help others.

- I can ________________________________
- I can ________________________________

This week I can __________ for others.

- I can ________________________________
- I can ________________________________

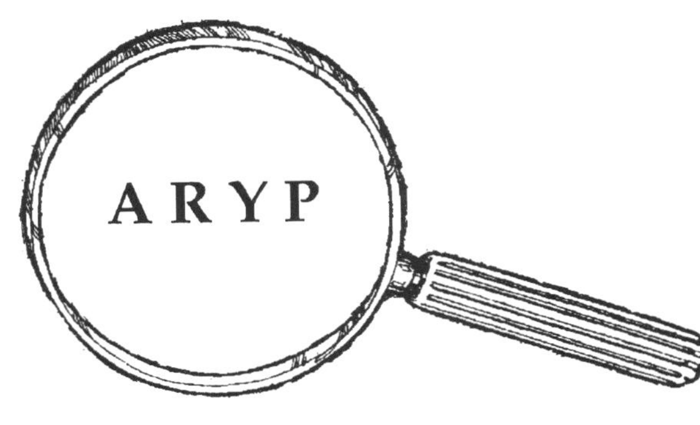

This week I can __________ with others.

- I can ________________________________
- I can ________________________________

I learned some things from the ________ today.

- I learned ____________________________
- I learned ____________________________

Pray
Give a gift
Call
Send flowers or balloons
Make a card
Get Better!
Visit and smile

Examine the story of the healing of the lame man more closely. **Read Acts 3:1-16** if you need help.

Every day people brought the man who was lame and lay him at the **(2 down)** of the Temple called the **(3 across)** Gate.

At 3 o'clock in the afternoon **(9 across)** and **(13 across)** were on their way to the **(4 down)** to **(16 across)**.

The man who was lame asked for **(14 down)**, but Peter said, "We have no **(10 down)** or **(15 across)**..., but in the name of **(17 across)** **(1 down)**, stand up and walk.

After the man was healed, the people saw him **(6 down)** and **(8 down)** and **(11 across)** **(12 down)**.

Peter said, "Why do you **(7 across)** at us. It is because of **(5 down)** in Jesus that this has been done."

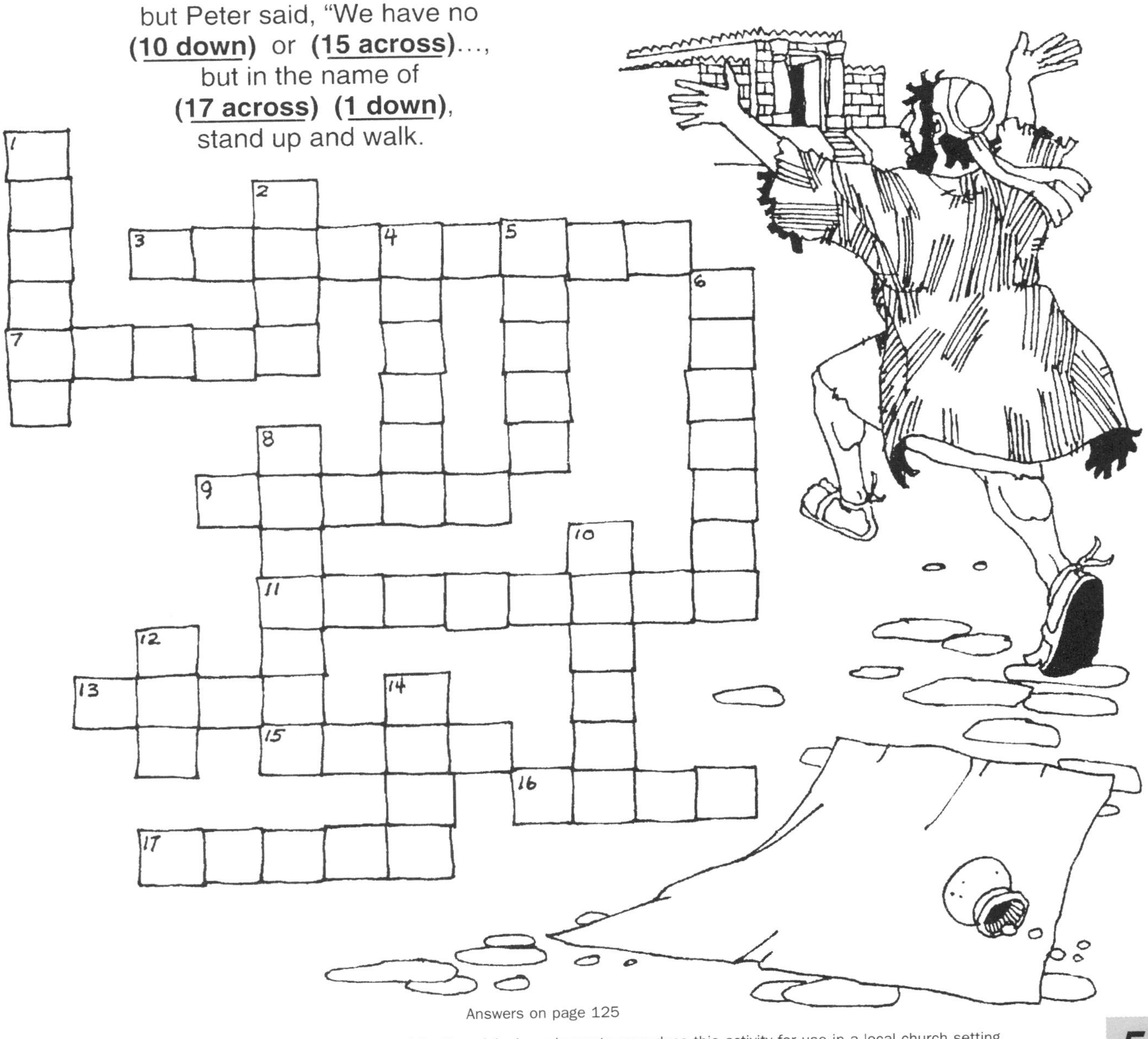

Answers on page 125

CIRCLE EVERYONE IN THE PICTURE WHO IS HELPING.

You Shall Be My Witnesses

Make a check (✓) beside each idea that is a way you can witness.
Add a line to make the check mark an X (✗) beside the ideas that would require special courage and strength from God.
Draw a circle (◯) around the marks beside each idea that you would like to try. Add some ideas of your own if you wish.

___ Invite a friend to Sunday school and worship.
___ Tell the truth even when it is easier to lie.
___ Look for ways to be helpful and kind at home.
___ Give money, clothes, food, or toys to help those in need.
___ Say no when the group suggests doing something that is wrong.
___ Tell a friend about Jesus and how Jesus wants us to live.
___ Invite someone who is unpopular to join an activity at school.
___ Make a card to send to someone who is sick.
___ Ask a friend who is swearing or telling dirty jokes to stop and explain why you choose not to do those things.
___ Do something kind for someone who is always picking on you.
___ ______________________________
___ ______________________________
___ ______________________________

Match each missionary with the person who is being helped.

On the Road With Philip

Read the story of Philip and the Ethiopian from your Bible in Acts 8:1-5, 26-40.

Locate the places that Philip traveled on the map from the Class Pak.

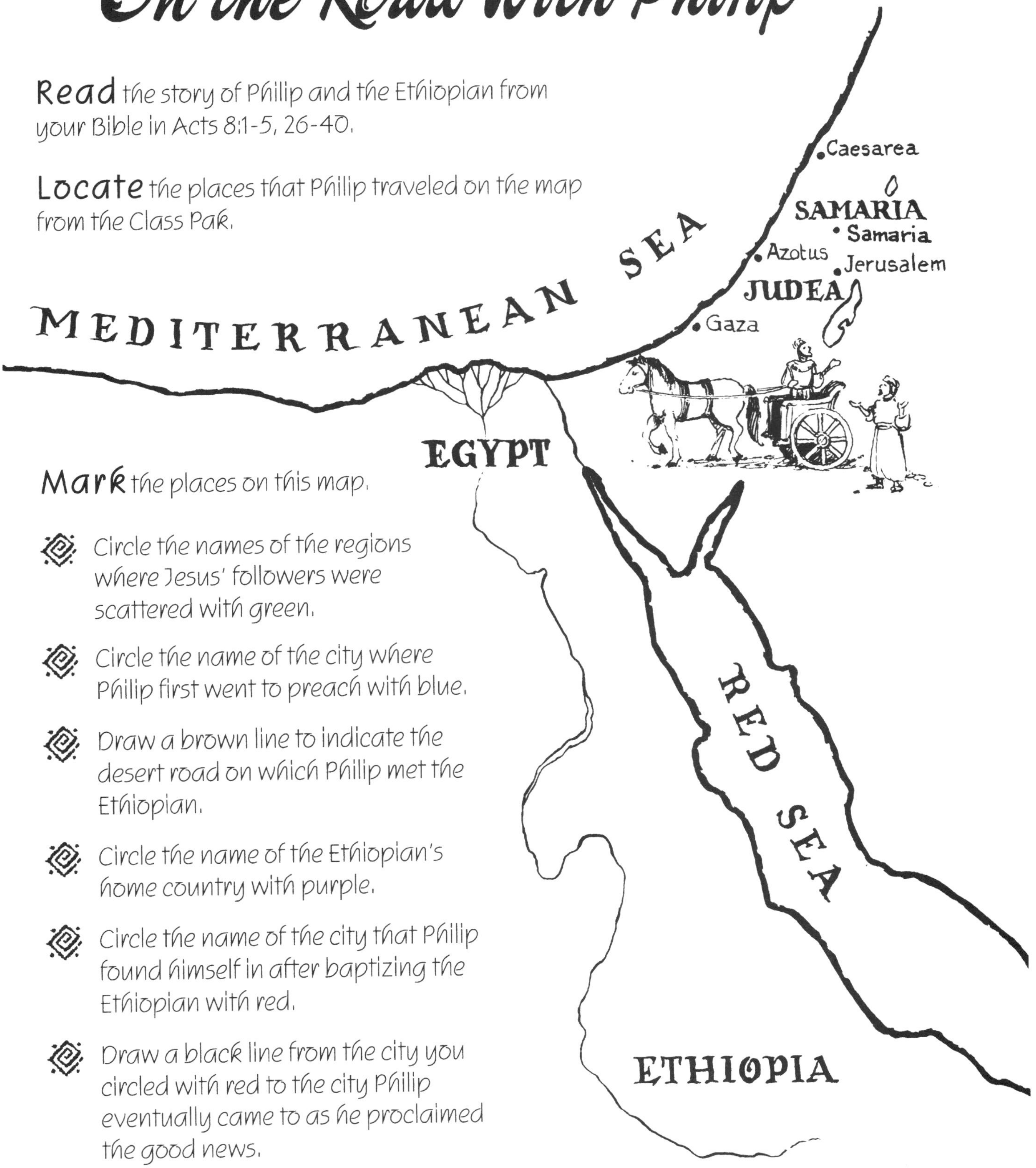

Mark the places on this map.

- Circle the names of the regions where Jesus' followers were scattered with green.
- Circle the name of the city where Philip first went to preach with blue.
- Draw a brown line to indicate the desert road on which Philip met the Ethiopian.
- Circle the name of the Ethiopian's home country with purple.
- Circle the name of the city that Philip found himself in after baptizing the Ethiopian with red.
- Draw a black line from the city you circled with red to the city Philip eventually came to as he proclaimed the good news.

Peter and Cornelius

"My name is Peter. Let me tell you about a dream I had. It helped me see things in a new way. One day I went up to the roof to pray. While I was there, I dreamed I saw a sheet filled with animals coming down from heaven. But they weren't just any animals. These were the animals that our Jewish law said we must not eat!

"Then a strange thing happened. I heard a voice say, 'Peter, eat.' Of course I refused. I had never broken the law. But the voice insisted, 'What God has called clean, you must not consider unclean.'

"When I woke up, there were three men outside looking for me. They had come to ask me to go to Cornelius's house. Cornelius was a Roman centurion, and we Jews were not supposed to visit the homes of Gentiles. But I knew that God wanted me to go. I began to understand what my dream meant.

"I had learned that God does not love one group of people more than another. And neither should I. When Jesus said 'Love one another,' he meant everyone. When he commanded that I preach the good news, he meant for me to include everyone—not just the Jews or the people who were just like me.

"Suddenly, I found myself telling Cornelius and all his people about Jesus. These Gentiles were filled with the Holy Spirit, just like the disciples were at Pentecost. And I baptized them just as Jesus wanted me to do.

"When I opened the door of Cornelius's house and walked in, I opened the door for the good news of Jesus to be told all over the Roman Empire. When I left, I prayed that I would be worthy of God's trust."

Based on Acts 10:1-48.

What's Your IQ?

Do you accept people and include everyone in activities?
Or, do you always hang around with the same people and don't accept others who are different?
Which of these people would be in your group of friends? Be honest!

5 *Definitely!* **3 *Maybe?*** **0 *No way!***

_____ a new kid in the neighborhood
_____ a person who is unable to see
_____ a foreign exchange student who knows little English
_____ a person who is homeless
_____ someone from a different church
_____ someone who sings out of key
_____ someone in a wheelchair
_____ a person who has a different color skin
_____ a person who lives in a poor part of town
_____ a child with only one parent
_____ a person who does not go to church
_____ a person who did not invite you to his or her last party
_____ a migrant worker
_____ a person in a lower grade
_____ a person who failed last year
_____ a person just like you
_____ someone named Peter who says, "God doesn't play favorites. You should accept all people equally."

Add your points to discover you IQ (Inclusiveness Quotient).

71—85 I'd like to be your friend—you're inclusive!

40—70 I can't be sure what you will do. You accept some and not others. It depends!

0—39 You've got work to do! Read Acts 10:1-48 again. What does God want you to do?

Draw Peter's dream.
Draw something you dream about

God, help me remember to share.
My Prayer Book
I am sorry, God.
I thank you, God, for friends.

We pray many kinds of prayers each day, depending on what is happening in our lives. Read the prayers here and identify what kind of prayer each one is.

Note: Some include two kinds of prayer!

a. Prayers of Praise

We give honor to God in prayers of praise. We show our joy for all God has done, and acknowledge God's power. Prayers of Praise may sometimes be called Prayers of Adoration.

b. Prayers of Thanksgiving

We say prayers of thanksgiving to say say "thank you" for the many things God has given us and has done for us.

c. Prayers of Petition

"To petition" means to ask for something. We are praying a prayer of petition when we ask God to provide the things we need or want. Prayers of Petition may sometimes be called Prayers of Supplication.

d. Prayers of Intercession

Intercessory prayers are prayers for the needs of *other* people. We become the community of faith and feel the support of other Christians when we pray for one another.

e. Prayers of Confession

When we confess the ways we have failed to live as God wants us to live, we say "I am sorry" to God. When we confess, we ask for forgiveness, and we promise to do better.

___ 1. Thank you, God, for loving me.

___ 2. God, when I sit by the water and look at your beautiful world, I am filled with joy.

___ 3. God, my grandmother is not feeling well today. Please be with her and help her to get well.

___ 4. I really want to be on the ball team, God. Help me do a good job at tryouts.

___ 5. God, I shouldn't have yelled at my brother today. Help me be more patient next time.

___ 6. I am taking a math test today, God. Help me remember what I studied last night.

___ 7. Thank you, God, for the food we have to eat.

___ 8. Our country needs you, God. Help our president make good decisions.

___ 9. God, you are wonderful!

___ 10. God, I broke Mom's vase today; and then I lied. Please forgive me. And be with me when I tell Mom the truth.

Happy Birthday,
Church!

On Pentecost Day, while the disciples were waiting in Jerusalem, they received a wonderful gift. Write the words from the side of the box on the lines below to discover what Peter told the people about this gift.

(Acts 2:38b-39)

Who did Peter say that God's promised gift was for? __________________

Find the hearts that are the same, then change them by coloring them different colors.

LIFE IN BIBLE TIMES

Directions: Imagine you are a kid living in Galilee during Jesus' ministry. That would be around A.D. 30. Try to answer the following questions; some may have more than one correct answer.

_____ 1. You would sleep on (a) the ground, (b) a thin mat, or (c) a bed.

_____ 2. Boys and girls would be treated (a) about the same, (b) a little differently, or (c) much differently.

_____ 3. If you were a boy, you would learn by (a) going to school, (b) working with your father, or (c) both.

_____ 4. You would be considered an adult member of the community around age (a) 13, (b) 15, (c) 18, or (d) 21.

_____ 5. Your family pet might be a (a) cat, (b) dog, (c) goat, or (d) both a and c.

_____ 6. Your family gets water from a (a) village well, (b) a stream or river, or (c) a spring.

_____ 7. Your diet would include (a) fish, (b) bread, (c) figs, (d) coffee, or (e) lamb.

_____ 8. Would you have any toys? (a) yes or (b) no

_____ 9. You would speak (a) Aramaic, (b) Greek, (c) Latin, (d) Olde English, or (e) Gaelic.

_____ 10. The scrolls in your home would be (a) the Scriptures, (b) about farming, (c) about other lands and places, or (d) good story books.

ANSWERS:
1. Probably (b), unless your family was very wealthy, then perhaps (c).
2. c
3. c
4. a
5. Most likely c. Goats are easy to care for and are a source of nutritious milk.
6. Any of these answers could be right, depending on where you lived.
7. All except d.
8. a
9. Certainly a (Aramaic) and possibly b (Greek), but probably not c (Latin). Definitely not any of the others.
10. None of the above. This is a trick question. Books and scrolls of all those kinds existed, but they were copied by hand and very expensive. Unless your family was extremely wealthy, you would have no books or scrolls at home.

TO MARKET, TO MARKET

You live in the Holy Land in Bible times. You are on your way to the market and need to think about what foods you can buy. Put a check next to any food you might find there.

Answers on page 126

COLOR THE PICTURE

MAKE A LIST

What does your family do on the Sabbath (Sunday)?

WORD SCRAMBLE

Unscramble these important words from today's Scripture.

D O L R (Jesus' title) ____________

A T A H S B B (a special day) ____________

V I D A D (a king) ____________

R I A N G (used to make bread) ____________

L E F I D (place) ____________

H A R S E S E I P (Jesus' enemies) ____________

FILL IN THE BLANKS

Use the words below to fill in the blanks.

grain	paralyzed	Sabbath
harm	help	Law
angry	happy	

The Pharisees were ____________ because Jesus and his disciples plucked ____________ on the ____________. They claimed Jesus was breaking the ____________. Then Jesus healed a man whose hand was ____________. This made the man ____________. Jesus said, "Which do you think God wants us to do, to ____________ or ____________ on the Sabbath?"

WHAT IS DIFFERENT?

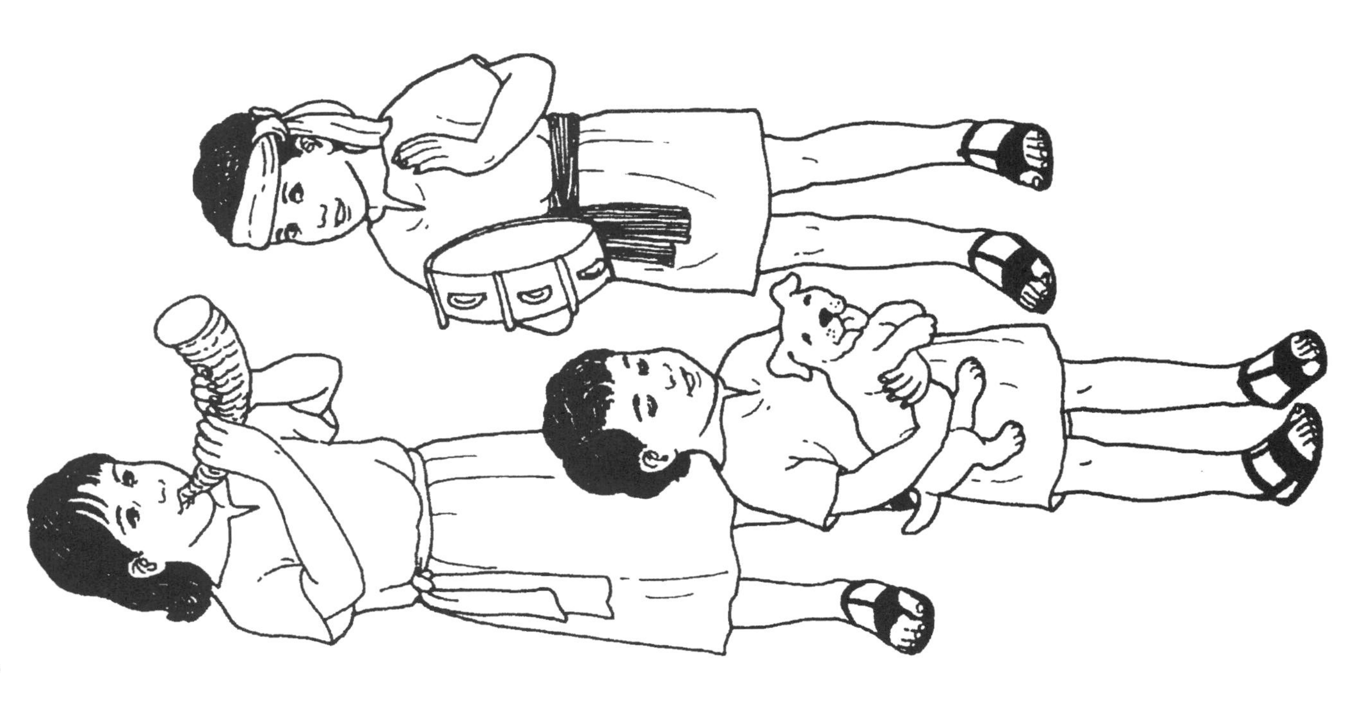

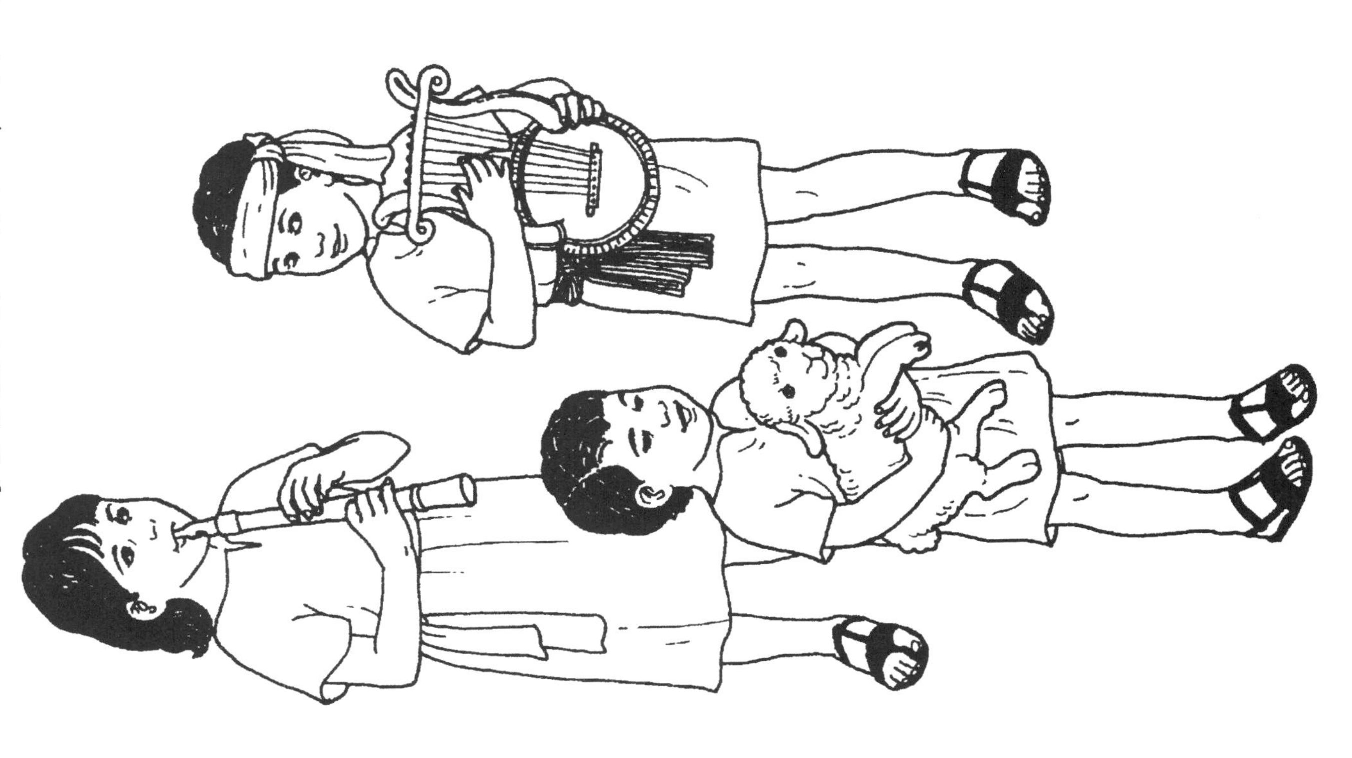

How many praise words can you find in these letters?

Praise Words
Glad
Joy
Love
Music
Praise
Psalms
Sing
Thanks
Worship

H	R	I	J	L	I	D	A	L	G
I	L	O	V	E	P	R	A	G	L
M	U	S	P	R	A	L	O	D	P
W	O	R	S	H	I	P	I	N	R
I	U	Y	H	M	U	S	I	C	A
P	S	A	L	T	S	A	U	S	I
T	H	A	G	K	S	L	P	R	S
J	O	N	W	O	R	M	Y	C	E
T	I	K	I	N	J	S	O	G	R
S	T	H	A	N	K	S	J	I	R

Help Samuel Find David

Find the path that Samuel must take to find the brother God has chosen to be king.

Can you find God's words in Samuel's path to find David? Be careful! The words do not always go where you might expect. Often they will turn corners!

The Lord does not see as mortals see; they look on the outward appearance, but the Lord looks on the heart.

1 Samuel 16:7c

Answers on page 126

In the Boat
The Storm
Wake Up!
Peace! Be Still!

HOW CAN I SHOW I HAVE FAITH?

FEELING FACES

What feeling do you think each face is showing? Name the feeling on the line below each face.

Draw two more faces showing feelings you have had this week. Name those feelings on the line below each face.

The person in the center of this page is entangled in the cares of life. To untangle this poor fellow, follow the lines from each care to one of the blanks at the bottom of the page. Fill the blank with the letter beneath the care. When all the cares are untangled, you will discover words to help you from becoming entangled in life's cares. Some letters are used more than once.

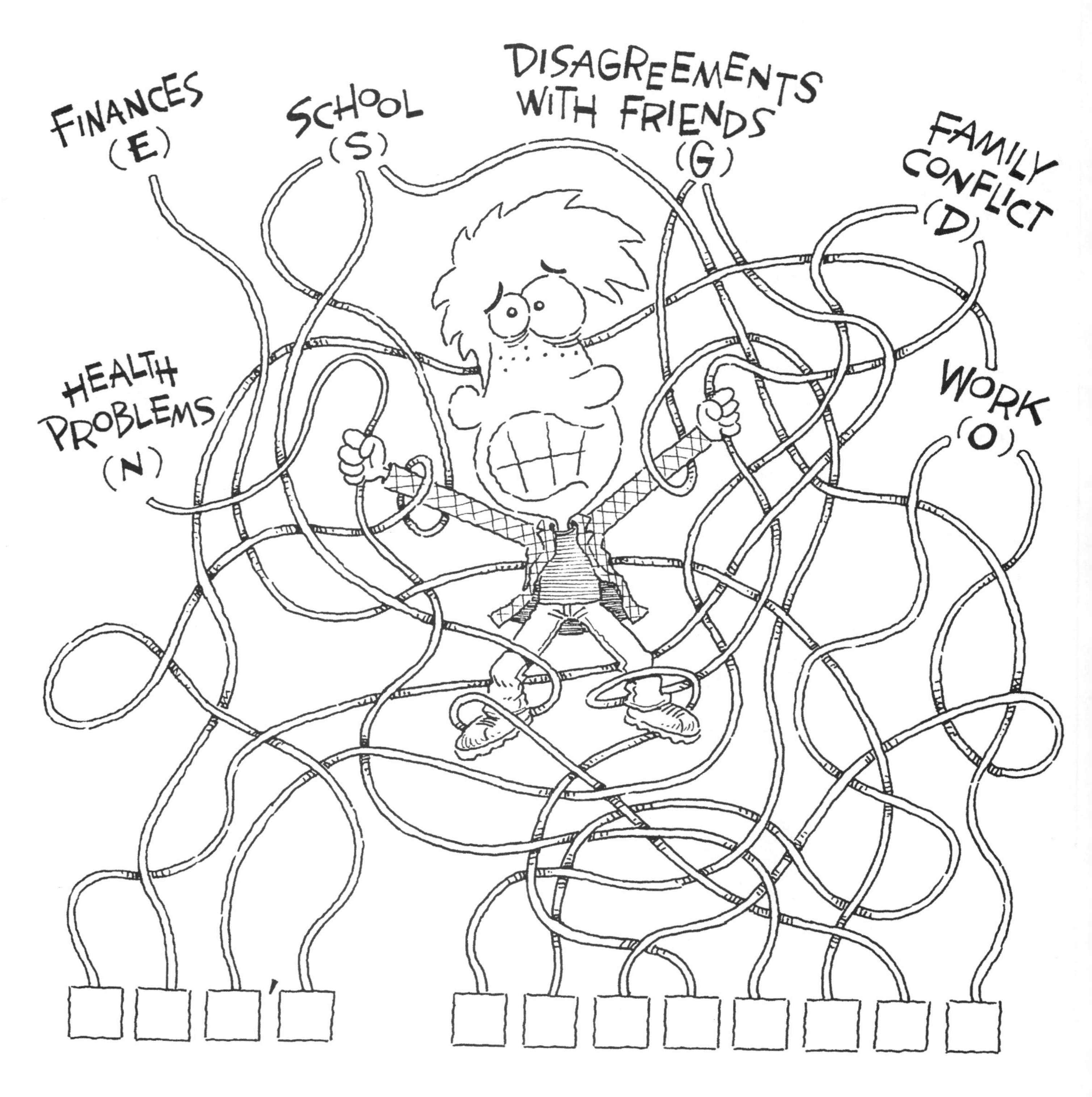

How Can You Help?

Find each number on the phone keypad. Then guess which of the letters is needed to find the message in each of the three phone numbers below. Don't give up! Keep guessing until you find the right letters to reveal the messages about telling the good news.

Example: The number 6 in the puzzle can be an M, N or O.

MNO
6

___ ___ ___ - ___ ___ ___ ___ ___ ___ ___ - ___ ___ ___ ___ ___ ___ ___ - ___ ___ ___ ___

9 4 8 - 6 3 7 7 9 6 8 - 8 3 5 5 4 6 7 - 4 2 7 3

Answers on page 126

Match worship
symbols from
Bible days
to now
Holy
Bible

Help David remember the events of his life. Unscramble the words to complete David's memories.
If you need help, look up the stories in your Bible.

__________ (Sualme) anointed me to be king.

[1 Samuel 16:13]

God gave me a gift for playing the _________ (ryle), I loved to write and sing ______________ (lpassm).

[1 Samuel 16:16, 23; Psalm 23]

My best friend was __________________ (onaJnhat).

[1 Samuel 18:1]

I was a _____________ (heerspdh).

[1 Samuel 16:19]

I first became the king of __________ (dJuha) and later became the king of all ______________ (rleIas).
[2 Samuel 2:4; 5:3]

My father's name was ___________ (sseJe).

[1 Samuel 16:19]

I brought the ________ ___ ___ ____________ (kar fo hte doLr) also called the _____ ___ _____ ___________ (rak fo eht ocnveatn) to Jerusalem.
[2 Samuel 6:17; Exodus 25:22]

I returned all of Saul's land to his grandson ______________ . (epMshhiobhte)

[2 Samuel 9:6-7]

I wanted to build a Temple in Jerusalem, but my son ___________ (loSmnoo) will build the Temple.

[1 Kings 5:1-12]

SAVE!

Answers on page 126

DRAW A PICTURE

Draw something about today's Scripture.

CONNECT THE DOTS

A place we like for a rest.

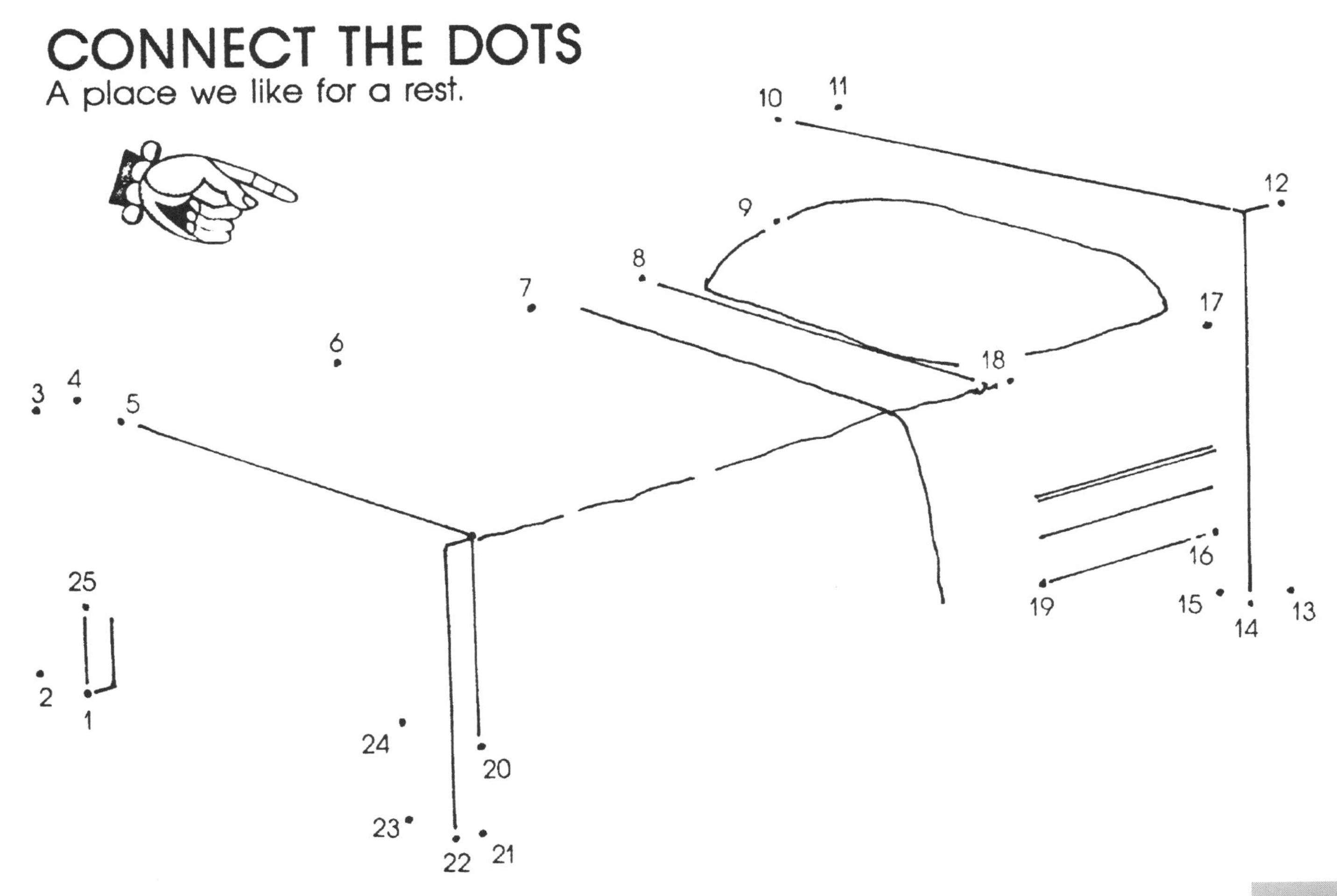

MAZE

Help Jesus and the disciples find a place to rest.

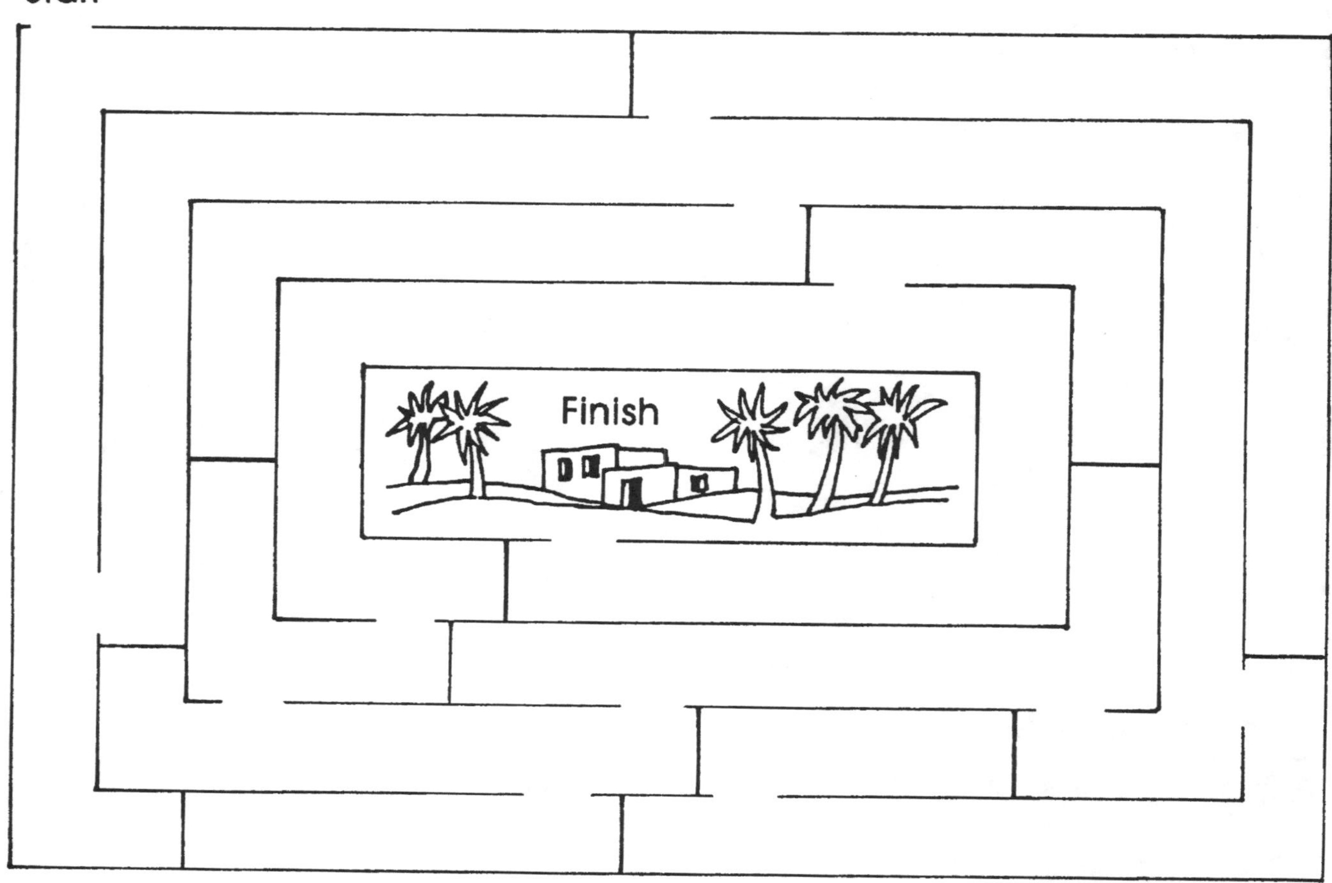

WORD SCRAMBLE

Unscramble these words from today's Scripture.

P S E H E ______________________

P E S T O L A ______________________

S T E R ______________________

T O B A ______________________

Y T I P ______________________

W R D O C ______________________

D R E P S H H E ______________________

Find the five loaves of bread and the two fish
that Jesus used to feed the crowd.
Can you tell the story?

Bread

Bread is a food common to people in all times and in all places. In Bible times bread and fish were eaten by even the poorest people. Everyone—then and now—understands the importance of bread for life.

It is no mystery that even during the time that Jesus lived, people spoke of bread as a symbol of life itself. Without bread, the people could not live. Bread became a symbol not only of physical life but of the spiritual life that comes from God.

Use your Bible to discover some of the ways bread has been used as a symbol of both physical life and spiritual life. Write a word or a phrase beside each reference to describe what is being described as bread.

Scripture	**Bread Describes**
Exodus 16:1-4a	______________________
Exodus 25:23-30 and 2 Chronicles 4:19	______________________
Matthew 6:9-13	______________________
Matthew 26:26-29	______________________
Luke 24:28-35	______________________
John 6:30-34	______________________
John 6:35, 48-51	______________________ ______________________

I AM BIG ENOUGH

Circle the pictures that show what you are big enough to do.

Identify some ways you can use your time and talent to make a difference at church and at home.

Example literally means *"to take out."*

An *example* is one that is set apart from others to show what the others are like.

A person who is an *example* is someone to be followed or imitated.

Color each space that has a word that begins with one of these letters: B K T O A F

As you find each word, write it in this space.

When you have found all the words, put the words in the right order. Write the Bible verse at the bottom of the page. Read Ephesians 4:32 in your Bible to fill in the missing words of the Bible verse.

____

____

Answers on page 127

Draw a line from each instrument to the people who might use it. Add some instruments of your own if you wish.

Five Kinds of Prayer

(1) Praise — Praise means that we recognize how great God is and we say how much we love God. In the Lord's Prayer the phrases "hallowed be thy name" and "for thine is the kingdom, and the power, and the glory forever" are words that praise God.

(2) Thanksgiving — Thanksgiving means that we recognize what God has given to us and done for us. We say "thank you, God."

(3) Confession — To confess is to tell God that we know we have done things that are wrong. When we confess, we also say "God, I am sorry." When we pray "forgive us our trespasses as we forgive those who trespass against us" in the Lord's Prayer, we are praying a prayer of confession.

(4) Intercession — Intercession is praying for someone else. Through prayers of intercession we may ask God to help someone, to comfort someone, or to be present with someone during a difficult time.

(5) Petition — Petition is telling God what we need. "Give us this day our daily bread" in the Lord's Prayer is a prayer of petition.

Match each of these prayers with the kind of prayer that best describes it.

___ 1. "Help my father find a job."
___ 2. "Thank you for loving me."
___ 3. "You are a wonderful God!"
___ 4. "Help me as I take my math test."
___ 5. "I'm sorry I broke mother's vase."
___ 6. "Your world is so beautiful, Lord."
___ 7. "Help Mrs. Jones get well."
___ 8. "I appreciate the food we have to eat."
___ 9. "Help me be a friend to Joe."
___ 10. "Help our country's President make good decisions."
___ 11. "Forgive my sins."
___ 12. "Help me to be picked for the ball team."
___ 13. "I thank you for the Bible."
___ 14. "You are so good to our church, God."
___ 15. "Help the missionaries tell people about Jesus."
___ 16. "Thank you for my Sunday school teacher."
___ 17. "God, I know you will always love me no matter what."
___ 18. "I am sorry I got so mad."

Bible Stories
I was glad when
they said to me,
"Let us go to the
house of the Lord!"
Psalm 122:1
Bible Stories
Bible Stories
Bible Stories

Sanctuary — a place set apart for sacred use. In the sanctuary Christians worship and experience the holiness of God.

Which of these pictures is most like the sanctuary in your church?

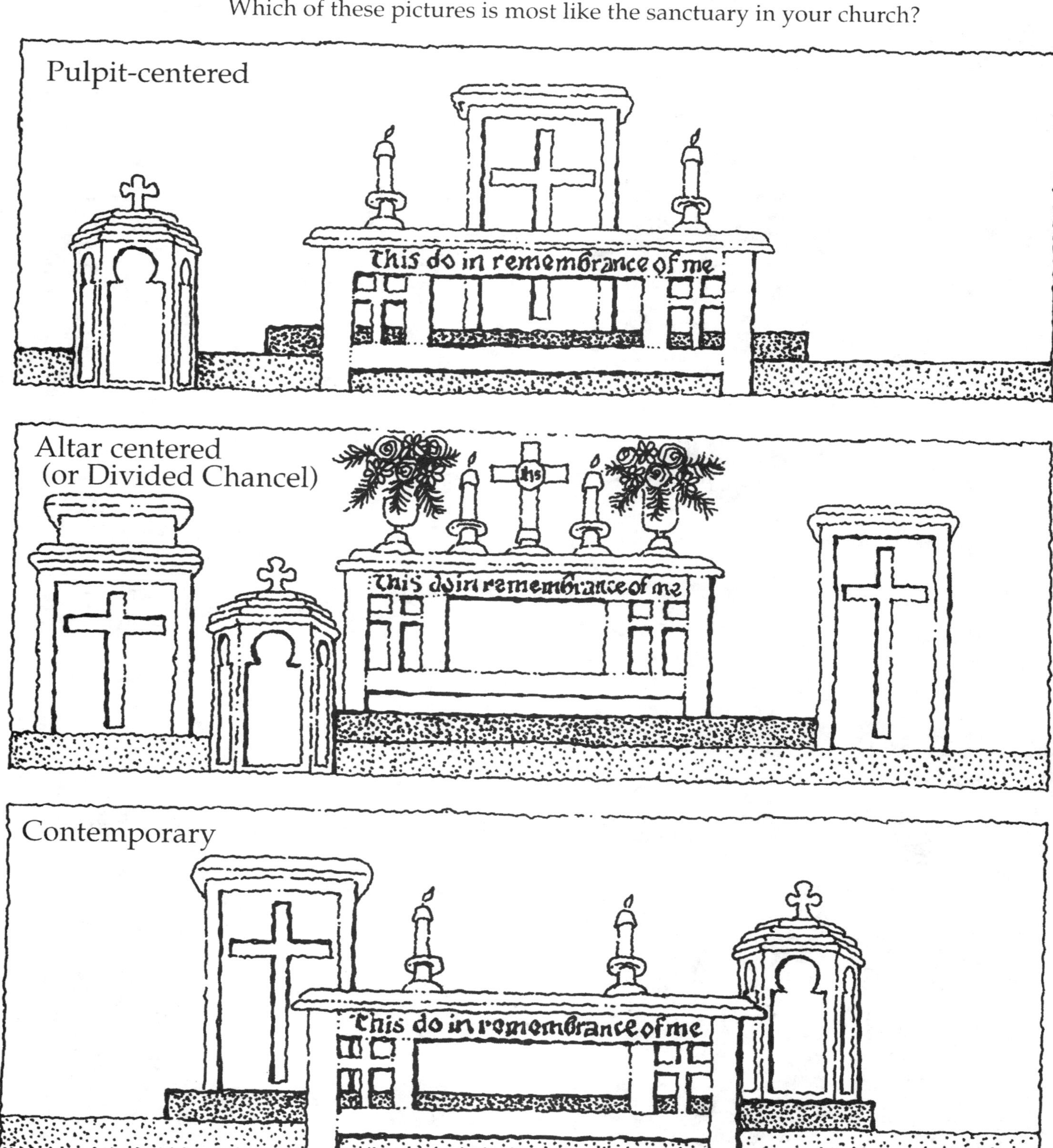

Can you find Jesus and some of his disciples?
You can recognize them by what they are wearing!

What Is the Bible?

The Bible has many names. The maze below shows some names for the Bible. Follow the path in the direction of the arrow with each name until you reach a description of the meaning of the name.

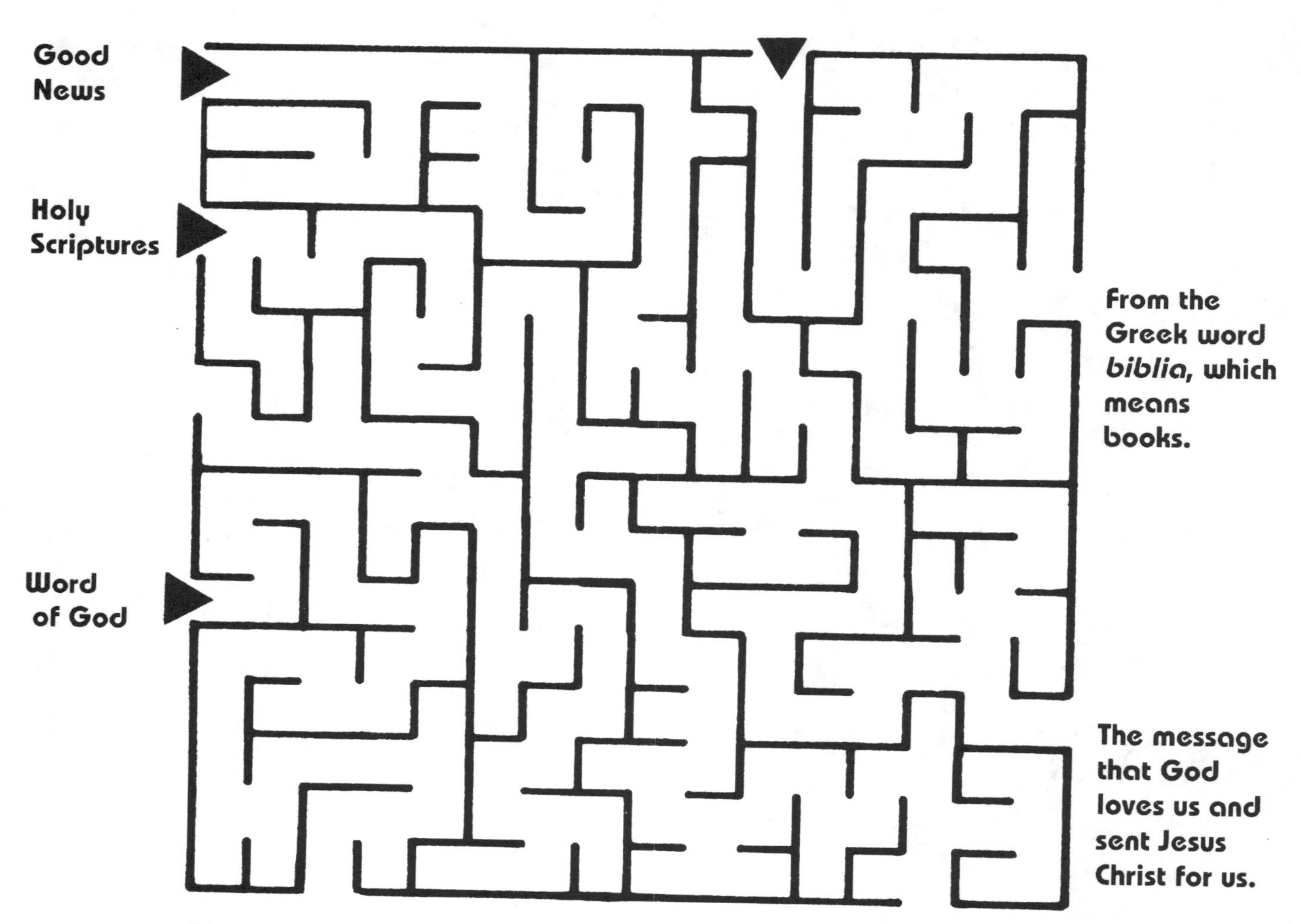

The Bible was written by people who were inspired by God. God speaks to us through the words of the Bible.

Scriptura **is Latin for writings. The English word** ***Scriptures*** **refers to sacred writings. The word** ***Holy*** **tells us that the writings come from God and deserve special respect.**

Answers on page 127

Things I Need and Things I Want

Whoever is kind to the poor
lends to the ________,
and will be repaid in full.
(Proverbs 19:17)

Describe a mission project students in your class have participated in. What did you do? Who did you help? How did you take part?

____

____

____

____

____

____

How is giving to the poor giving to God?

____

____

(Look up Psalm 24:1;
Matthew 25:34-40 for clues!)

Those who despise their
neighbors are sinners,
but ___________ are those who are
kind to the poor.
(Proverbs 14:21)

What kind of attitude should we have when we help others?

"I wish they would take care of themselves."

"It's no big deal. I'll do it if I have to."

"I am happy to serve God by helping others."

List things that your church shares with those in need in your community.

1. ______________________
2. ______________________
3. ______________________
4. ______________________
5. ______________________

Put a check beside each project you have participated in. Circle the number of each project you would like to be a part of in the future.

Those who are _______________
are blessed,
for they share their bread with
the ____________.
(Proverbs 22:9)

Who is the most generous person in your church? Explain why.

____

because ______________________

____

____

____

______________________________.

What can you learn
from each of these people?

Pick a Proverb

These proverbs are from the *Good News Bible.*

Proverbs are wise sayings that were written to help people learn how to live. Pick the proverb that can be a guide in each of these situations.

Melissa lost her mother's favorite bracelet. She had not asked her mother if she could borrow the bracelet. Melissa thought, *Maybe I could just tell her someone stole it.* ______________

Tom's friend said, "You don't have to pay for that candy bar. Come on, I'll show you how to sneak out of the store with it." ______________

"I'm tired of going to school," said Brian. "I'm not going to do my homework this week." ______________

Jessica wants to be a doctor. She knows it will be hard work. She's not sure she is good enough. ______________

Jason thinks his Dad is old-fashioned. He decides he just won't listen when his father tells him how he should behave.

____

Jacob's teacher said, "It is rude to push ahead of others in the line. You should learn to wait your turn." ______________

Jennifer saw the other kids throwing trash on the ground around the picnic table. But she remembered that her parents had said it was each person's responsibility to keep the city clean. Jennifer picked up the trash and put it in the trash can. ______________

Answers on page 127

Ways to Serve

Circle the pictures that show ways you can serve God now.

Can you find Mark 9:35b in the letters below? Follow the directions for each line. Write the words of the Bible verse on the blank lines.

1. Cross out all the A's and all the B's.	A B A W H A O B E A V B E R A
2. Cross out all the Z's and all the C's.	Z C W C Z C C Z A N C Z T S Z
3. Cross out all the S's and all the L's.	S L S T L L L S S L O S L L S
4. Cross out all the Y's and all the R's.	Y R Y R B Y Y Y R R R E Y R Y
5. Cross out all the J's and all the D's.	F J J D I D D J D J R S J D T
6. Cross out all the E's and all the K's.	E K K E M E E K U K K E S T K
7. Cross out all the O's and all the Q's.	Q Q Q O O B O Q O O Q E Q O Q
8. Cross out all the H's and all the U's.	S H U E H U U H R U V H A N T
9. Cross out all the N's and all the I's.	N I I I N N O N I F N I N N I
10. Cross out all the V's and all the F's.	V F F V A V F V V L F V L V F

Esther became the queen of Persia. How many crowns can you find for Esther hidden in the picture?

Jewish Man Shows Disrespect for King's Advisor!

(Esther 3:1-4)
(9 down) ____________, a Jewish resident of the kingdom, refused to bow down before the king's advisor, (10 across) ____________. When asked for an explanation, he said, "I worship only (12 down) ____________."

Official Plans Oppression of a Religious Group

(Esther 3:2, 5-6)
King (5 across) ____________, advisor (1 across) ________ was infuriated to discover that one of the king's (8 across) __________ at the king's gate refused to bow down. The king's advisor has made plans to destroy the servant (2 down) ____________ and all of the (4 down) __________ throughout the kingdom.

1, 2, 3, 4, 5, 6, 7, 8, 9, 10, 11, 12, 13, 14

Queen Acts Courageously!

(Esther 4:11-17; 7:9-10)
Although she faced possible danger of losing her own life, Queen (6 down) ____________ appealed to the king to spare the lives of her people. When the king realized what was happening, he had (7 down) ____________ hanged on the gallows he had built for (13 across) ____________.

Jews Celebrate Holiday!

(Esther 9:18-19, 24-28)
The Jews set aside two days each year to remember the courage of Queen (11 across) __________ that saved them from destruction. They call their holiday (14 across) __________, which comes from the name Pur, which recalls (3 down) ________ ________ that was cast to determine the date of their ordered destruction.

Answers on page 127

MAZE
Help the children find Jesus.
START

Use these clues to help you find Mark 10:14. What did Jesus say when the disciples tried to keep the children away from him?

Clue 3: The number 10 after the name Mark tells which chapter in the Book of Mark you need to find. The big numbers that divide the book into sections are chapter numbers. Turn to Chapter 10 of the Book of Mark.

Clue 4: The number 14 after the colon (:) tells which verse you need to find in Mark 10. The smaller numbers within each chapter are the verse numbers. Find verse14 in Chapter10 of the Book of Mark.

Congratulations!

You have found Mark 10:14.

When Jesus saw this, he was

_______________ and said to them,

"_______ the _____________

_____________ __________ _____ ______."

Now find these stories about Jesus in your Bible. Remember: Stories about Jesus are in the Gospels, the first four books of the New Testament.

Matthew 3:13 Jesus came from Galilee to be _______________.

Mark 14:32 Jesus went to a place called Gethsemane to

__________.

Luke 6:8-10 Jesus healed a man who had a _______________ __________

John 10:11 Jesus said, "I am the _______________

____________________."

Answers on page 128

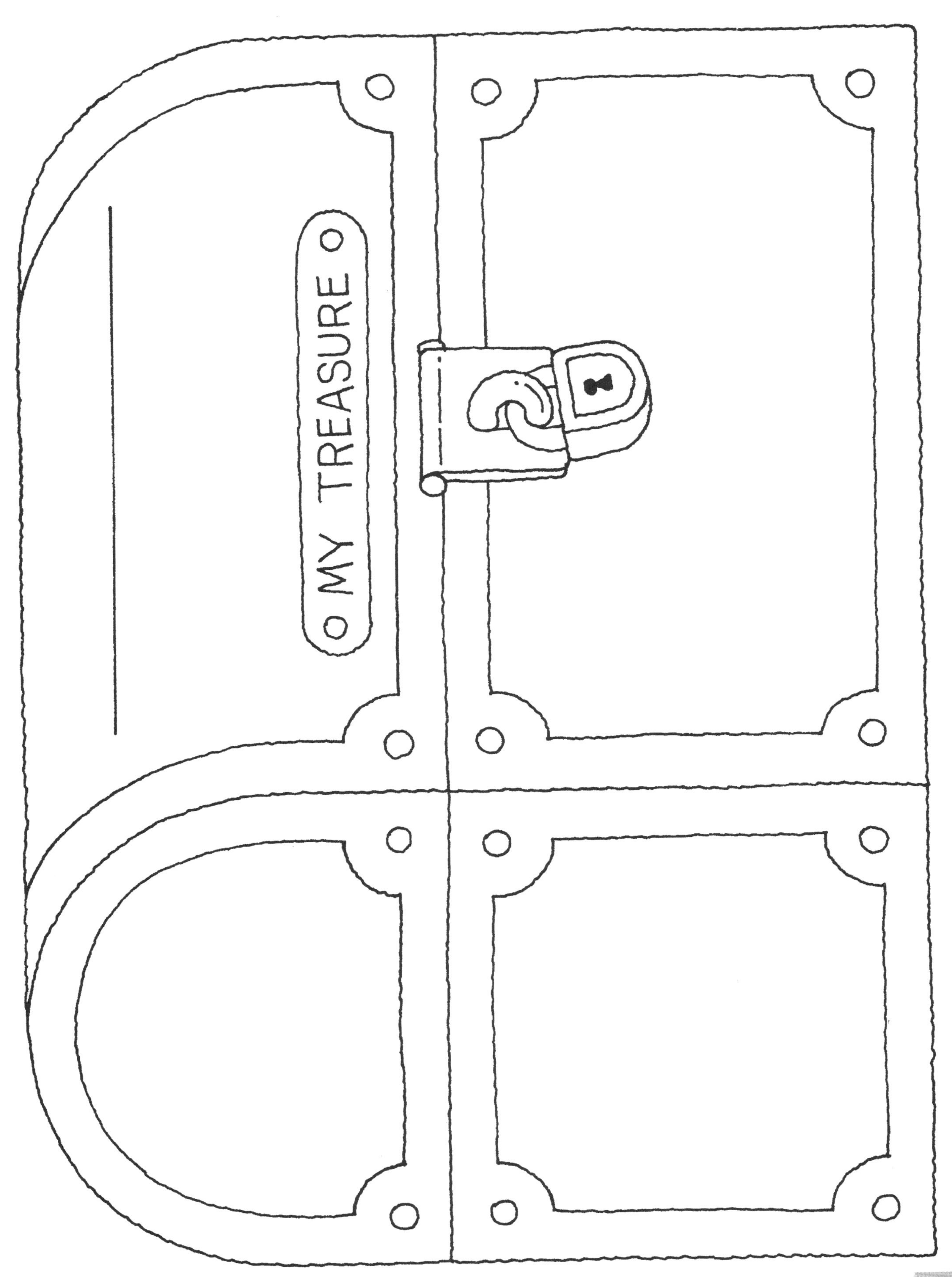
MY TREASURE

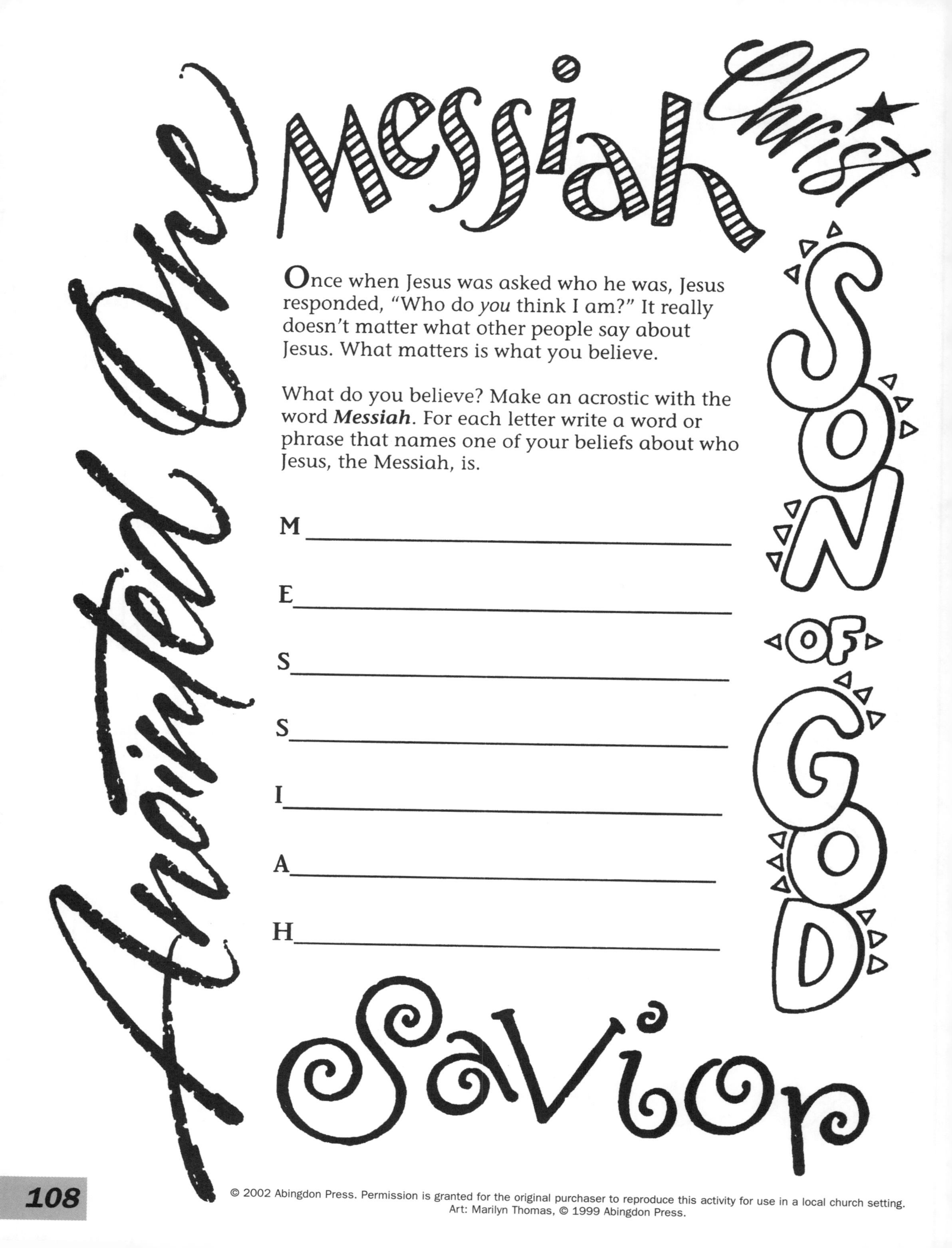

Once when Jesus was asked who he was, Jesus responded, "Who do *you* think I am?" It really doesn't matter what other people say about Jesus. What matters is what you believe.

What do you believe? Make an acrostic with the word ***Messiah***. For each letter write a word or phrase that names one of your beliefs about who Jesus, the Messiah, is.

M ____________________

E ____________________

S ____________________

S ____________________

I ____________________

A ____________________

H ____________________

Name each season of the year as you follow the path from Spring to Winter.

Start at the beginning. Find your way through the maze back to the beginning. What do you find that God created?

For a clearer picture, you may want to color in the lines along the path you followed.

Answers on page 128

DRAW A PICTURE

Draw a picture from today's Scripture.

HELP THE MAN FIND JESUS

Help Bartimaeus, the blind man who wanted to be healed, find Jesus.

Jesus, the Healer

Read each story about Jesus, the healer. Then fill in the chart to show the many ways Jesus healed and the ways people responded.

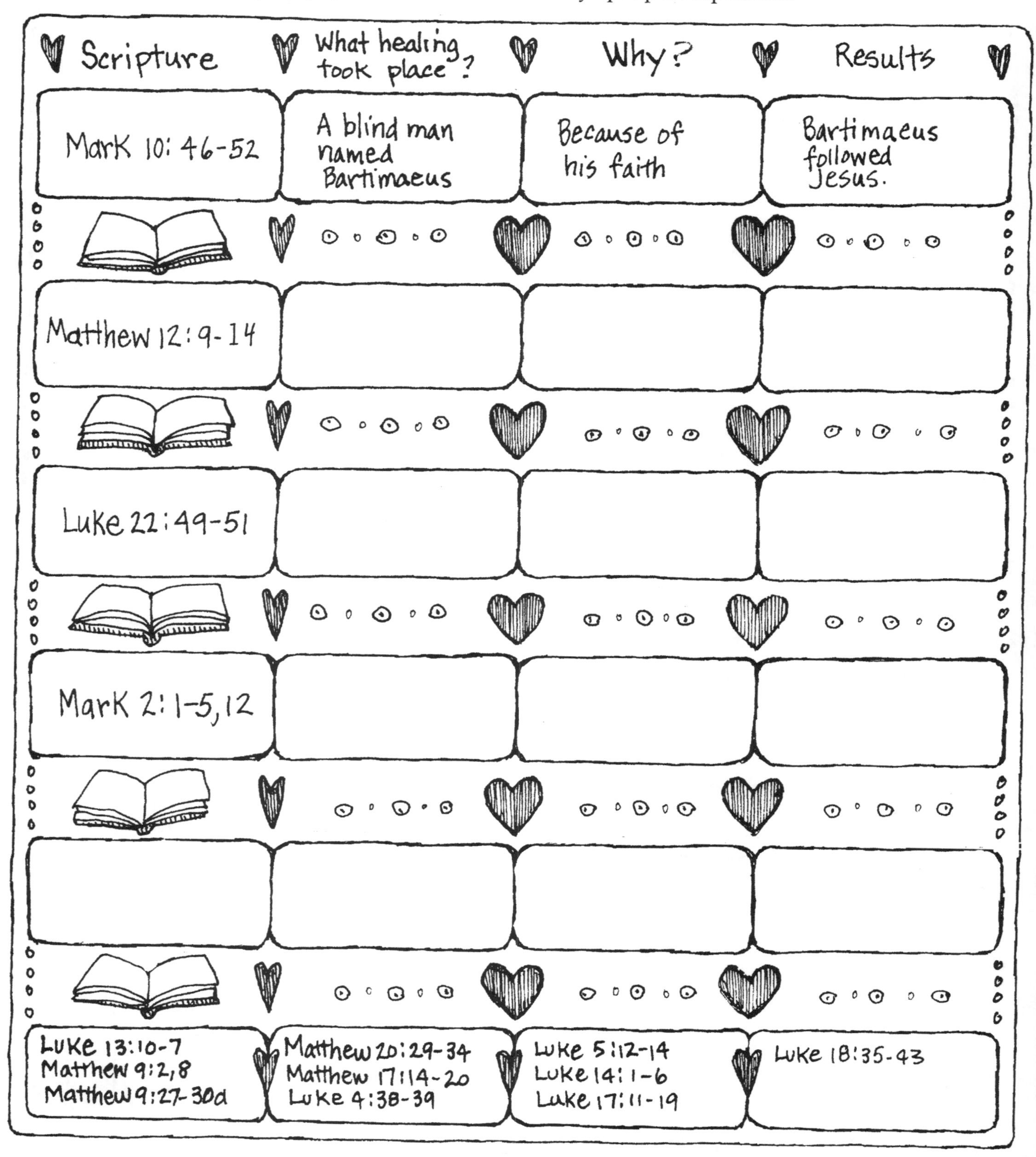

Scripture	What healing took place?	Why?	Results
Mark 10:46-52	A blind man named Bartimaeus	Because of his faith	Bartimaeus followed Jesus.
Matthew 12:9-14			
Luke 22:49-51			
Mark 2:1-5,12			

Luke 13:10-7 Matthew 9:2,8 Matthew 9:27-30a	Matthew 20:29-34 Matthew 17:14-20 Luke 4:38-39	Luke 5:12-14 Luke 14:1-6 Luke 17:11-19	Luke 18:35-43

Choose Loving Actions

Mark a red *X* through the picture that shows unloving actions. Color the pictures that show loving actions.

Here is a code with a symbol for each letter of the alphabet. Use it to decode the message that follows.

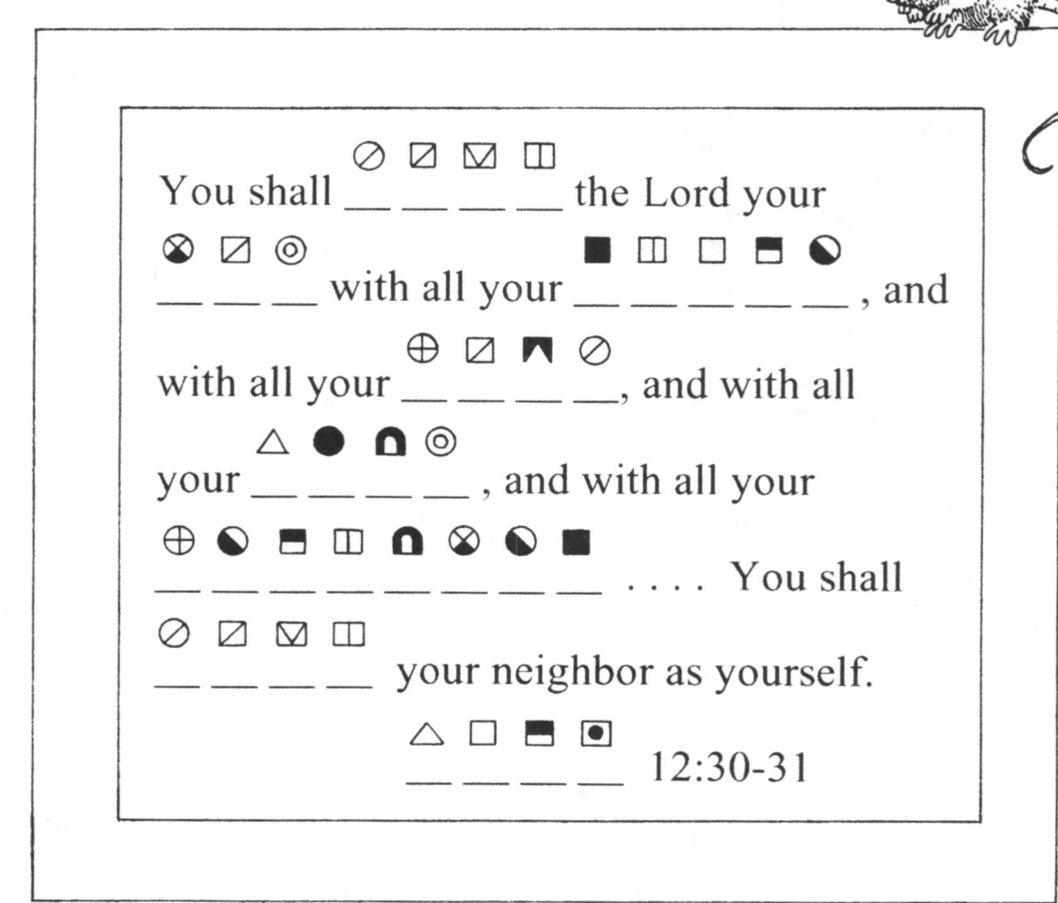

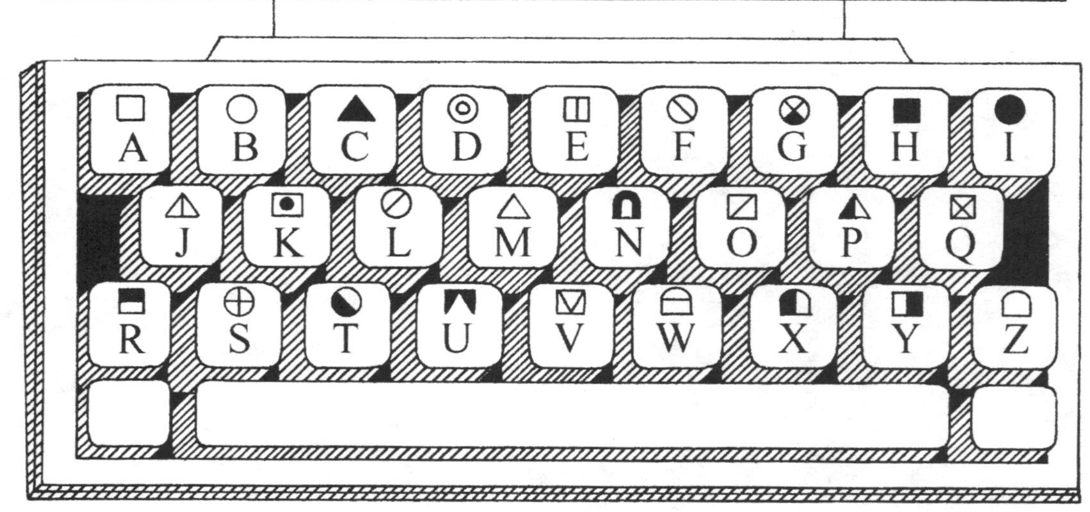

- Why do you think these verses are a "mystery" to some people?
- Is it difficult or hard to follow these rules all the time, every day?
- Why do you think Jesus said this was the greatest commandment?
- Talk about your answers with a friend and your teacher.
- Now use the code to write a message for your parents. Choose a favorite Bible verse or simply say "I love you."

Answers on page 128

Discover Acts of Kindness

Draw a circle around the people you see who are being kind.

How many acts of kindness did you find?

Glean the Words

During Bible times, poor people gleaned grain left in the fields of the wealthy farmers. Can you glean the twenty-two words left in the letters below? The words can be found by reading from left to right or top to bottom.

WORDS TO GLEAN

RUTH
MOAB
BETHLEHEM
WIDOWS
HEBREWS
HARVEST
FIELDS
NAOMI
BOAZ
OWNER
KINDNESS
FOREIGNER
PEOPLE
DEEDS
LORD
HUSBAND
MARRIED
OBED
RESTORE
LOVE
GLEAN
GRAIN

T	G	R	U	X	F	O	R	E	I	G	N	E	R
P	L	U	N	G	I	P	D	E	E	D	S	H	E
B	E	T	H	L	E	H	E	M	N	P	R	U	S
H	A	H	X	O	L	E	L	O	V	E	S	S	T
A	N	G	F	R	D	B	L	A	E	S	Y	B	O
R	M	G	P	D	S	R	Y	B	O	A	Z	A	R
V	D	R	F	N	P	E	O	P	L	E	M	N	E
E	M	A	W	A	O	W	Z	F	O	B	E	D	R
S	W	I	D	O	W	S	N	F	O	W	N	E	R
T	C	N	F	M	A	R	R	I	E	D	D	G	E
E	U	D	K	I	N	D	N	E	S	S	P	R	L

Answers on page 128

I Am Old Enough

Circle each picture that shows something you have done to help at church or at home.

What Can I Give?

It takes the gifts of everyone in the church to make the church work. What gifts can you give? Check each gift that you are giving with a check mark (✓). Then draw a star (☆) beside the ones you will think about doing later.

I can give gifts to my church.

Around the church I can

____ help my teacher clean the class space
____ sharpen pencils for the sanctuary
____ design a bulletin board for the hallway
____ pick up litter in the churchyard
____ be a greeter on Sunday mornings
____ wash the toys in the nursery
____ dust the pews in the sanctuary
____ help prepare the bread and juice for Communion
____ ________________________________
____ ________________________________

In worship I can

____ attend, listen, and sing
____ sing in the children's choir
____ be an acolyte
____ pray
____ read the Scripture
____ participate in a special program
____ be an usher
____ ________________________________
____ ________________________________

For the world I can

____ sweep the wheelchair ramps
____ pack clothes for donations
____ help serve food to people who are homeless
____ sing at a nursing home
____ invite someone to Sunday school and worship
____ send cards to missionaries
____ pray
____ ________________________________
____ ________________________________

What Would You Do?

What is wrong in each picture on the left? Draw a line to the picture on the right that shows the best thing to do.

HUNT AND FIND

Sometimes it is hard to know the truth about something. Find the letters T-R-U-T-H in the picture!

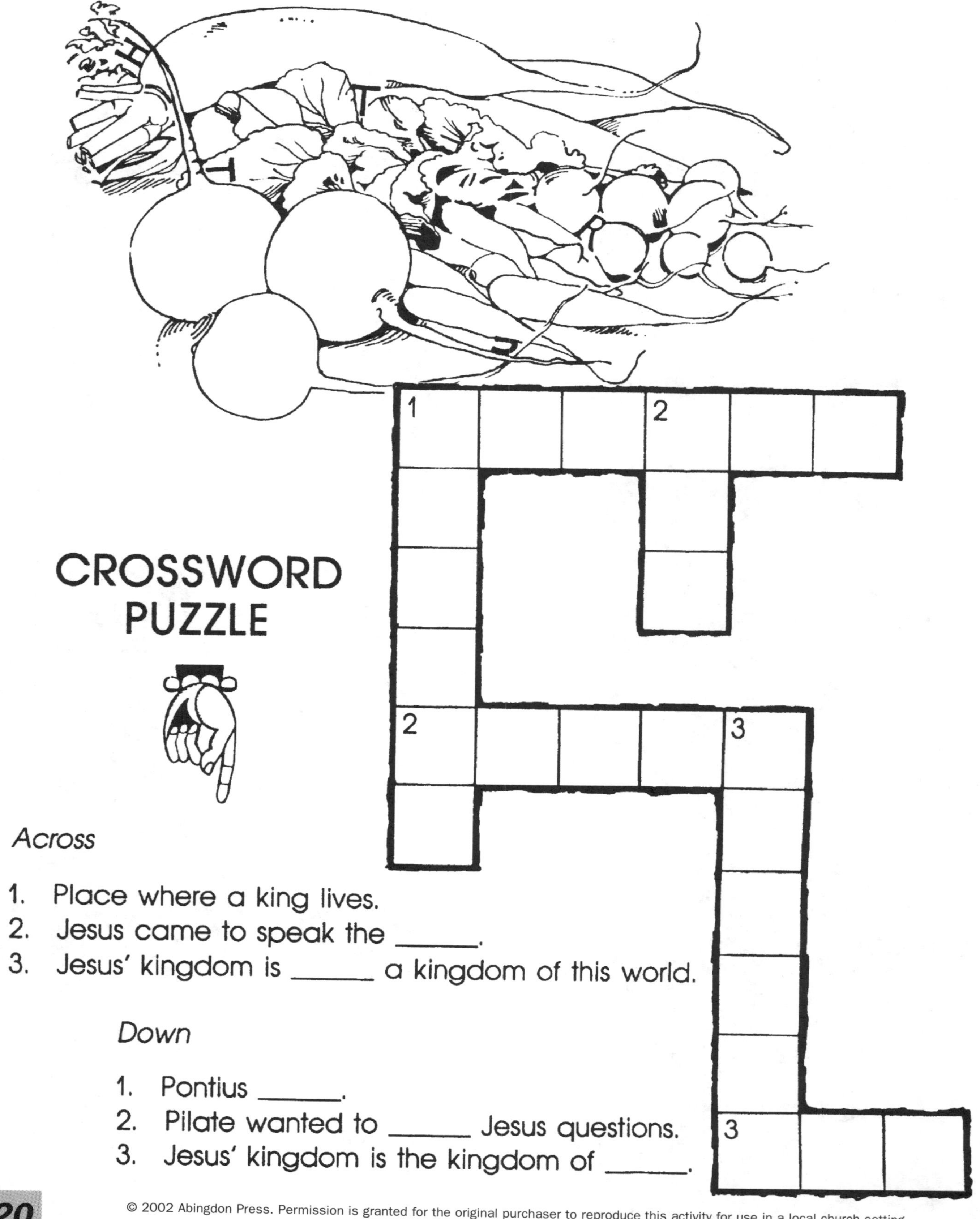

CROSSWORD PUZZLE

Across

1. Place where a king lives.
2. Jesus came to speak the ______.
3. Jesus' kingdom is ______ a kingdom of this world.

Down

1. Pontius ______.
2. Pilate wanted to ______ Jesus questions.
3. Jesus' kingdom is the kingdom of ______.

Index

Lectionary, Year B

Scripture

Old Testament

New Testament

Puzzle Answers

M 1. The last letter in the name of the animal that is a male sheep.
E 2. The second letter in the name of the animal with antlers.
S 3. The first letter in the name of the reptile that stays cool.
S 4. The fifth letter in the name of the animal that is similar to a grasshopper.
E 5. The third letter in the name of the animal that flies.
N 6. The second letter in the name of the animal that is long and has no legs.
G 7. The first letter in the name of the animal that has a "beard."
E 8. The second letter in the name of the animal that makes wild honey.
R 9. The fourth letter in the name of the animal that has four pairs of legs.

Now read Mark 1:6. Name two things John wore and two things John ate.

John wore **camel's hair** and **leather belt**.

John ate **locusts** and **wild honey**.

Page 6

Names for the Messiah

dfeluWnro luCosnroe
Wonderful Counselor

gythMi odG
Mighty God

ltgniseErva trheFa
Everlasting Father

cnirPe fo ceePa
Prince of Peace

hhpeedrS
Shepherds

What other names do you know for Jesus?

______________ ______________

______________ ______________

Page 8

"Let's **G**o now," the shepherds said to
One another. "Let's go to Bethlehem."
s**O** they went quickly, and they
foun**D** Mary and Joseph and the child, who was lying in the manger.
Whe**N** the shepherds saw this, they
mad**E** known what had been told them about this child.
All **W**ho heard it were amazed at what
the **S**hepherds told them.

Reading down, what do the letters you filled in spell? **Good News**

Who is the good news about? **Jesus**

Page 12

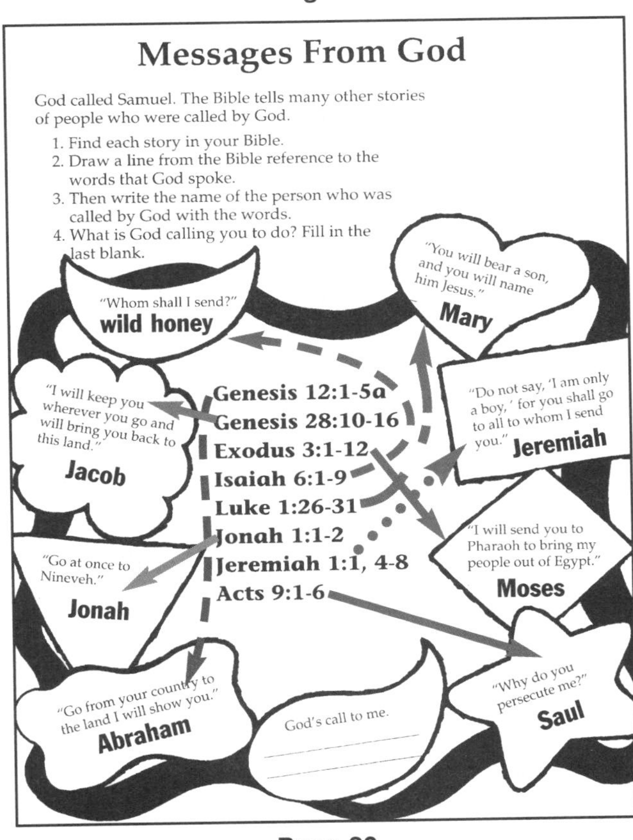

Page 20

Page 24

Circle the words below that name ways you can reach out to other people to show them that you care about them.

Compliment	Interact	Ignore	Reject
Speak	Care	Help	Give
Disapprove	Love	Hate	Tattle
Include	Frown	Accept	
Smile	Share	Tease	

Can you add some other words to circle? ____________ ____________

Fill in all the spaces in the letters below that contain O's. Who does Jesus love and want us to reach out to? ____________________

EVERYONE

Page 26

Page 32

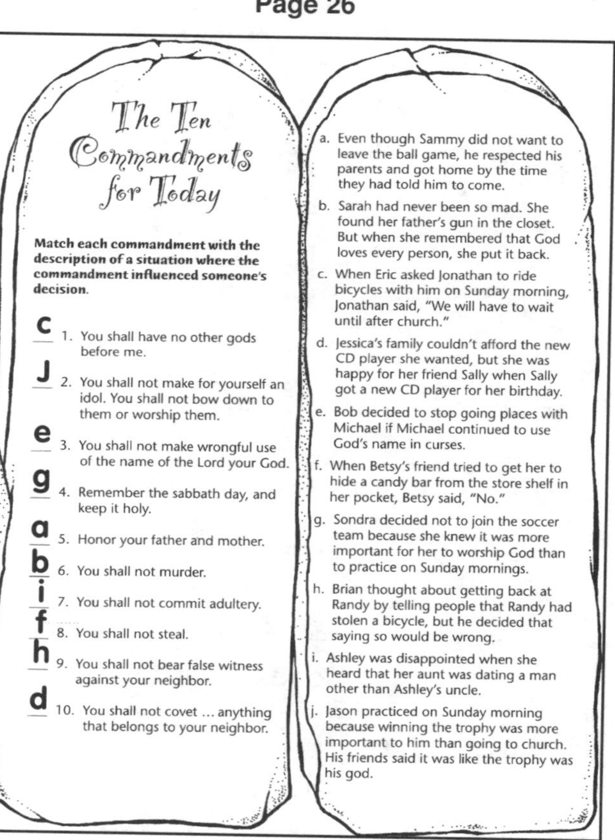

The Ten Commandments for Today

Match each commandment with the description of a situation where the commandment influenced someone's decision.

c 1. You shall have no other gods before me.

J 2. You shall not make for yourself an idol. You shall not bow down to them or worship them.

e 3. You shall not make wrongful use of the name of the Lord your God.

g 4. Remember the sabbath day, and keep it holy.

a 5. Honor your father and mother.

b 6. You shall not murder.

i 7. You shall not commit adultery.

f 8. You shall not steal.

h 9. You shall not bear false witness against your neighbor.

d 10. You shall not covet ... anything that belongs to your neighbor.

a. Even though Sammy did not want to leave the ball game, he respected his parents and got home by the time they had told him to come.

b. Sarah had never been so mad. She found her father's gun in the closet. But when she remembered that God loves every person, she put it back.

c. When Eric asked Jonathan to ride bicycles with him on Sunday morning, Jonathan said, "We will have to wait until after church."

d. Jessica's family couldn't afford the new CD player she wanted, but she was happy for her friend Sally when Sally got a new CD player for her birthday.

e. Bob decided to stop going places with Michael if Michael continued to use God's name in curses.

f. When Betsy's friend tried to get her to hide a candy bar from the store shelf in her pocket, Betsy said, "No."

g. Sondra decided not to join the soccer team because she knew it was more important for her to worship God than to practice on Sunday mornings.

h. Brian thought about getting back at Randy by telling people that Randy had stolen a bicycle, but he decided that saying so would be wrong.

i. Ashley was disappointed when she heard that her aunt was dating a man other than Ashley's uncle.

j. Jason practiced on Sunday morning because winning the trophy was more important to him than going to church. His friends said it was like the trophy was his god.

Page 40

Genesis 17:1-8
A covenant between **God** and **Abram**

Genesis 21:25-32
A covenant between **Abraham** and **Abimelech**

Exodus 34:1-10
A covenant between **God** and **people**

Genesis 31:43-46, 51-52
A covenant between **Laban** and **Jacob**

1 Chronicles 11:3
A covenant between **David** and **elders**

Exodus 19:5-6a
A covenant between **God** and **Israelites**

Genesis 9:8-17
A covenant between **God** and **Noah**

Genesis 12:1-2
A covenant between **God** and **Abram**

Psalm 132:11-12
A covenant between **God** and **David**

Jeremiah spoke for God when he said that God would make a new covenant with the people. Read Jeremiah 31:31-34. Then write the new covenant from verse 33 here.

I will write it on their hearts; and I will be their God, and they shall be my people.

Page 44

Each of these fourteen words about Lent can be found in the search two times. Which one can you find three times?

Lent	Hosanna (three times)
Palms	King of the Jews
Holy Week	Rooster
Jerusalem	Denarius
Cross	Holy Spirit
Last Supper	Disciples
Crucifixion	Good Friday

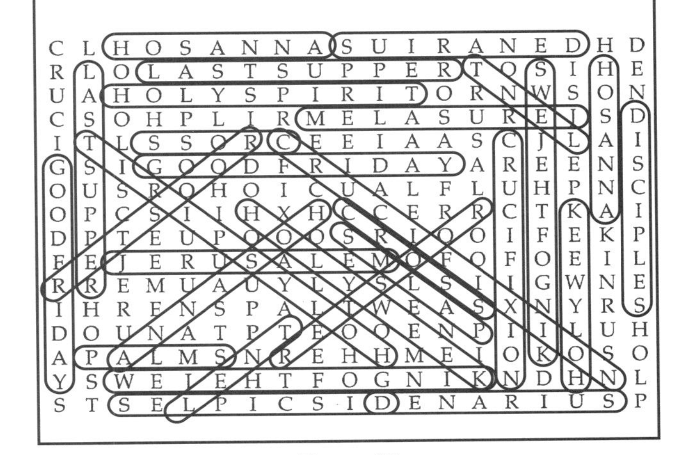

Page 46

Page 49

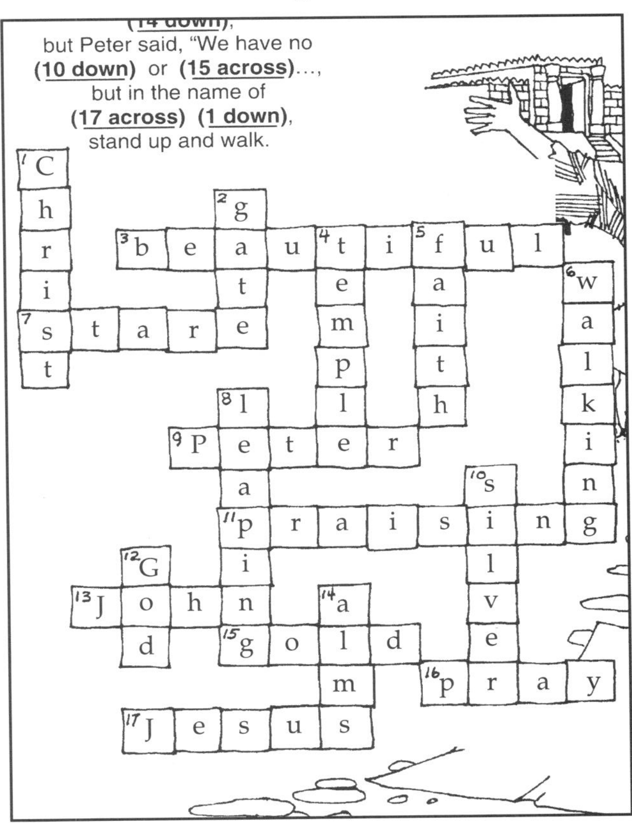

Page 55

Page 69

Can you find God's words in Samuel's path to find David? Be careful! The words do not always go where you might expect. Often they will turn corners!

ETV
MHELOR
NQNDD
MMSOE
NEB
SNA
AOF
TDC
SEW
EATC
SMORT
GHAK
MLJ
DSTM
SEE
UUT
LHK
TEY
SL
EOO
RK
ONO
NTI
JHP
EOK
MUTH
DWON
ARD
GAD
LPT
PF
ESR
AQA
RETD
ANCES
HBF
MUT
CTV
HRB
ELU
ORW
DAAX
LOOKSO
BGYNL
JTCO
HLZH
EHEA
CLR
NOT

The Lord does not see as mortals see; they look on the outward appearance, but the Lord looks on the heart.

1 Samuel 16:7c

Page 74

Page 80

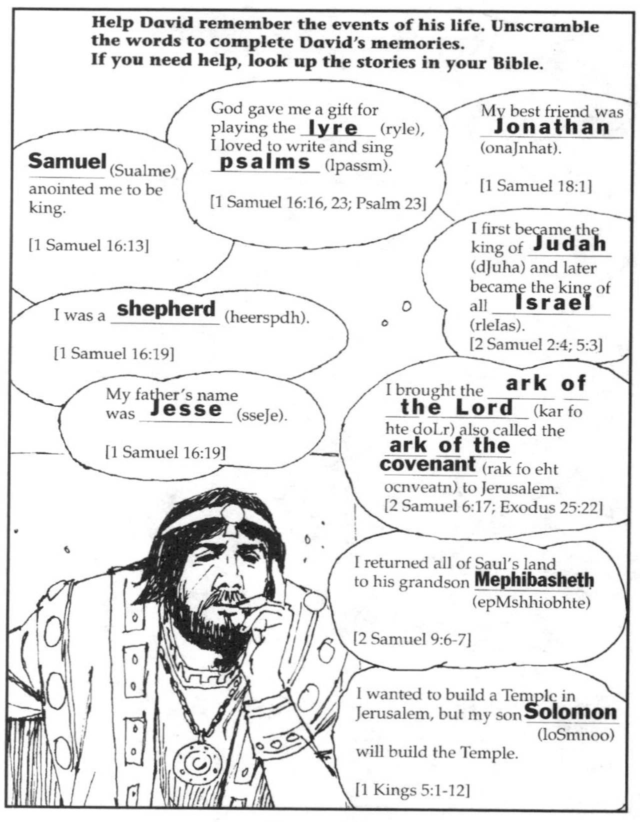

Page 82

As you find each word, write it in this space.

When you have found all the words, put the words in the right order. Write the Bible verse at the bottom of the page. Read Ephesians 4:32 in your Bible to fill in the missing words of the Bible verse.

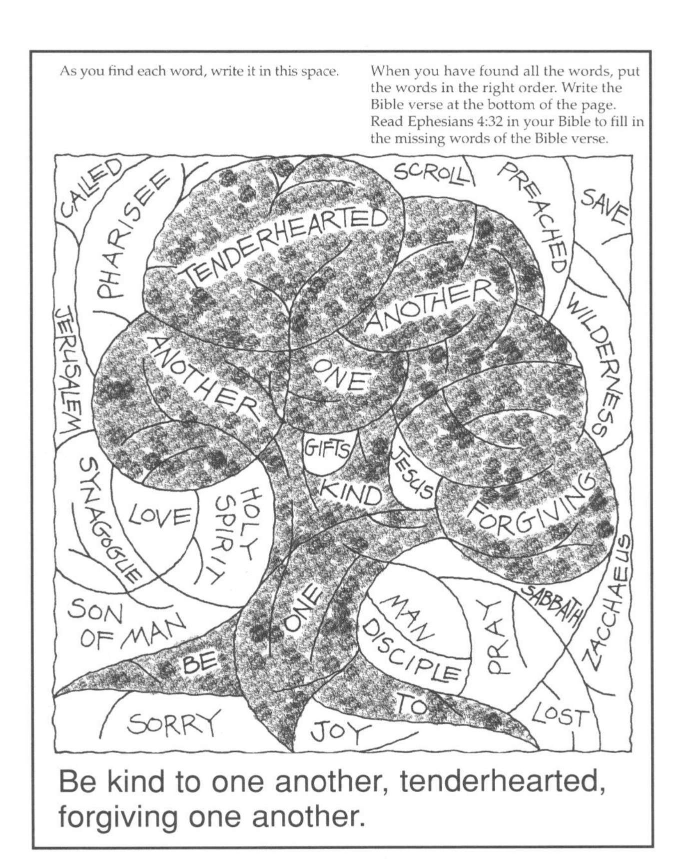

Be kind to one another, tenderhearted, forgiving one another.

Page 90

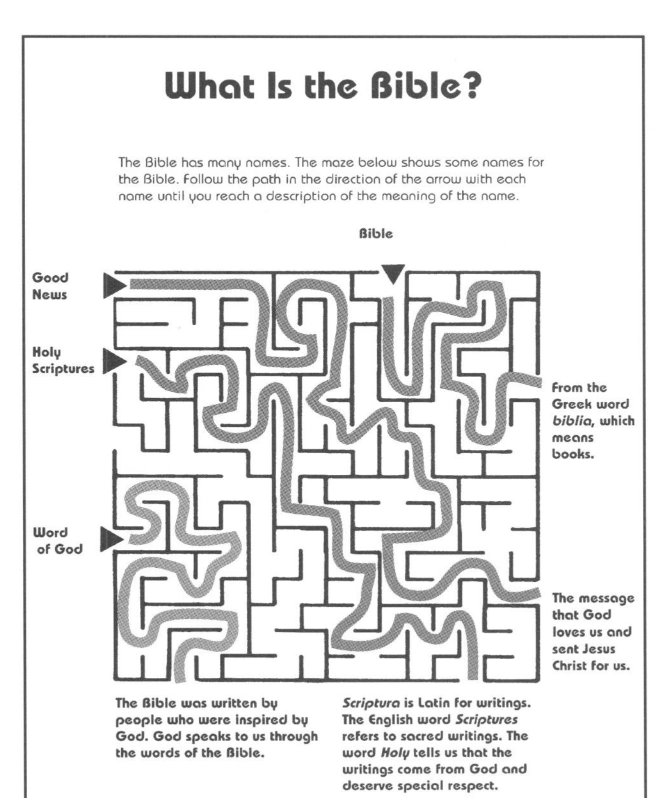

What Is the Bible?

The Bible has many names. The maze below shows some names for the Bible. Follow the path in the direction of the arrow with each name until you reach a description of the meaning of the name.

The Bible was written by people who were inspired by God. God speaks to us through the words of the Bible.

Scriptura **is Latin for writings. The English word** ***Scriptures*** **refers to sacred writings. The word** ***Holy*** **tells us that the writings come from God and deserve special respect.**

Page 96

These proverbs are from the *Good News Bible*.

Proverbs are wise sayings that were written to help people learn how to live. Pick the proverb that can be a guide in each of these situations.

Melissa lost her mother's favorite bracelet. She had not asked her mother if she could borrow the bracelet. Melissa thought, *Maybe I could just tell her someone stole it.* Proverbs 4:24

Tom's friend said, "You don't have to pay for that candy bar. Come on, I'll show you how to sneak out of the store with it." Proverbs 4:15

"I'm tired of going to school," said Brian. "I'm not going to do my homework this week." Proverbs 4:13b

Jessica wants to be a doctor. She knows it will be hard work. She's not sure she is good enough. Proverbs 4:25

Jason thinks his Dad is old-fashioned. He decides he just won't listen when his father tells him how he should behave. Proverbs 23:25

Jacob's teacher said, "It is rude to push ahead of others in the line. You should learn to wait your turn." Proverbs 15:31

Jennifer saw the other kids throwing trash on the ground around the picnic table. But she remembered that her parents had said it was each person's responsibility to keep the city clean. Jennifer picked up the trash and put it in the trash can. Proverbs 4:1

Page 100

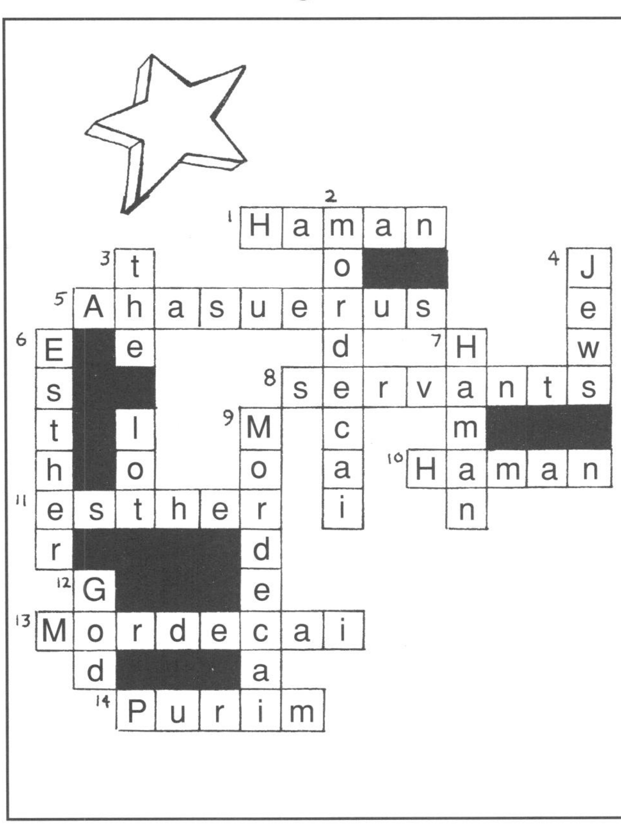

Page 104

Page 106

Page 110

Page 114

Page 116